Working
for
Yourself

First published in Great Britain in 1987
by Ward Lock Limited, 8 Clifford Street,
London W1X 1RB
An Egmont Company

All addresses and telephone numbers were accurate at time of going to press.

Designed and produced by Templar Publishing Ltd
107 High Street, Dorking, Surrey RH4 1QA
Typeset by Templar Type

Printed and bound in Great Britain
by R.J. Acford, Chichester, Sussex

British Library Cataloguing in Publication Data

Anslow, Maurice
    Working for yourself.—(Ward Lock reference).
    1. Small business—Great Britain   2. Self-employed—Great Britain
    I. Title
    658'.041'0941   HD62.7

ISBN 0-7063-6613-1

Working for Yourself

Maurice Anslow

Ward Lock Limited · London

Contents

Preface 6

1. Why work for yourself? 7

2. What kind of business? 11

3. Starting up 17

4. Planning ahead 23

5. Raising finance 31

6. What should you charge? 39

7. Advertising and marketing 45

8. Terms of trading 54

9. Keeping the books 58

10. Dealing with the VAT man 65

11. Using an accountant 71

12. Using a solicitor 79

13. Dealing with the tax man 86

14. Insurance and pensions 94

15. Business premises 101

16. Employing staff 109

17. Help and information 118

Preface

There has never been a better time for anyone in Britain to set up in business for themselves. After years of post-war industrial decline, the 1980s have seen a return to an atmosphere of enterprise and entrepreneurialism. Many people are now convinced that unless the country encourages self-employment and the creation of small businesses, it is failing to put down the roots of future economic growth.

Much of the change in attitudes has been as a response to the problems of high unemployment and the decline of traditional industries. The economy has to find new business ideas, and the people to run them who have the energy and vision on which tomorrow's prosperity depends.

This rediscovery of enterprise philosophy is something of a gamble. Apart from creating the best possible conditions in terms of financing, taxation and counselling, there is very little a government can do to ensure that an 'enterprise culture' succeeds. By its nature the success of a system which stresses initiative and risk-taking is dependent on the individual.

This book is for all people who have felt the first stirrings of the enterprise spirit, but who may not be familiar with the details and practical considerations involved in going into business on their own.

Maurice Anslow

1. Why work for yourself?

Everyone who wants to set up their own business has to ask themselves some searching questions about their reasons for taking such a risk – what are their motivations, strengths and weaknesses? It is one thing to believe that you are cut out to be your own boss and quite another to have the fortitude, thoroughness and good luck which will be required in order to succeed.

Indeed, the first thing you should ask yourself before deciding to become self-employed or start your own small business is whether you are prepared to fail – and try again? One in three small businesses fail within their first year. Over half will never survive as long as ten years. Although Britain's self-employed have doubled in number to around 3 million between 1980 and 1987 it would be a mistake to assume that all these first-timers in business are thriving.

If you are not worried about the stigma of failure, you are already half-way towards your goal of having your own successful business. Remember, experience shows it is only often on a second or third attempt that the entrepreneur finally hits on an idea that works.

Why am I doing this?

The difference between the security which comes from a regular job or even a dole cheque, and the lonely – sometimes desperate – world of working for yourself is enormous.

So ask yourself just why you want to be your own boss. Most people who start their own businesses have experienced being someone else's employee. Typically they feel frustrated at having to succeed on other people's terms. Very often the need for independence is not a major factor. This is an important point. If you are contemplating working for yourself because of a 'negative' reason, you are heading for trouble. Successful self-starters usually have a much more positive reason for wanting their independence. They will already be natural hard-workers. What they want is to work hard for themselves.

Am I ready for the challenge?

Establish the personal characteristics you possess which might be of value when working for yourself. Little more needs to be said about the ability to work hard. Perhaps equally important is a willingness to listen to others and take advice. Many people fail in self-employment through sheer pig-headedness. The 'know-it-all' is typical of many in this area: they invariably achieve little and usually blame anything or anybody other than themselves for their failure.

The fact that you are reading this book already suggests you are not that type. But go out of your way to take advice. Listen to bankers, accountants, friends and other people in self-employment or running small firms. Join local business clubs, read the business press, make use of government advisory schemes. Do anything but lock yourself away in isolation and fail to achieve your goal through sheer ignorance.

What experience do I have?

How experienced are you in the particular skill, craft, trade or profession in which you are proposing to start up a business? Many people will start up a particular business just because it represents something totally different from their previous employment. Running a village Post Office or small off-licence can look relatively idyllic to someone who has spent years slaving in an office or factory.

But don't plunge straight into a totally new activity without satisfying yourself that you are familiar with the special skills and demands which the business will require. Consider whether you need re-training or to do a great deal of swotting up before you are fully prepared to embark upon your new venture.

Consider whether you will be taking too much upon yourself. A classic mistake of business starters is that they underestimate the workload and overestimate their personal skills. It is rare for anyone to be everything from craftsman to book-keeper, tax expert to general dogsbody. Even if what has attracted you to self-employment is the idea of being 'on your own', it may be that you are more likely to succeed by bringing in a partner with complementary skills.

The risks and the rewards

Since there is a very high risk of failure in any new business venture you must be confident that you can bounce back, both personally and financially, from such a defeat. The cost of failure could be high and include:

- Total loss of personal savings.
- Appropriation of personal assets used as security on bank loans. This could mean your own home.
- Personal bankruptcy if you have not traded as a limited liability company.
- Damage to self-respect and future prospects.
- Possible damage to health.

Even supposing you don't fail, be prepared for a new set of problems which will not have arisen in your previous full-time employment or unemployment. These will include:
- Irregular income, particularly at first.
- Longer working hours and disruption to family life.
- The need to master new details like tax planning and legal requirements.
- Loneliness if you have been used to working with a large number of other people.
- Added worry and uncertainty.

The rewards of running your own business can be enormous. You are very likely to be making more money than was ever possible being someone else's employee. You are independent and more or less at liberty to progress your business just as it suits you. You have a sense of personal achievement which many of your friends in regular staff jobs know they can never experience.

Do I have the money?

There are no hard and fast rules about the capital required to start a business. Many multi-million pound businesses have been started on just £100 and a space on the dining room table. It depends on the type of business and whether it requires a great deal of capital equipment, such as machinery or vehicles. It will also depend on your personal financial position and whether you need to raise 'working capital' just to pay your wages.

Few businesses start up without some kind of loan and although there is plenty of money available for people with good ideas, banks will not even provide the smallest loan without security of some type. Ultimately the amount you borrow is determined by how much security you are prepared to put up, and also by your ability to 'service' the loan repayments by the cash flow of your business. A banker will want to see detailed projections which assure him that your business looks capable of repaying the loan. He will also want to see that you are confident enough about your idea to back it with some of your own cash – at least 10% of the total amount you need to start up. Raising money by offering your own house as security is the usual route preferred by most bankers, although there is obvious risk involved for the borrower. Banks can, and do, throw people out of their homes when they default on their loans.

Raising finance is discussed thoroughly in chapter 5, but at this point it is enough to say don't go into business with inadequate financial resources. 'Under capitalisation' is one of the most common reasons for business failure and if you have to delay going into business for yourself until you have amassed more personal savings, then do so.

2. What kind of business?

In setting up a business you have three structures to choose from; sole trader, partnership or limited liability company.

The majority of people registering as 'self-employed' are sole traders. In fact, over one third of all VAT-registered businesses in Britain today are classed as sole traders. Partnerships are, in effect, little different from sole trader in a legal sense and simply involve the sharing of responsibility for the business between two or more individuals. Forming a limited company can be done from the beginning, but is more usually the course chosen for a rapidly growing sole trader or partnership business which requires its own identity and protection under the law.

Sole trader

Setting up as a sole trader is a relatively straightforward affair. Typically you will be starting your business in a small way in your own home, in which case you are not likely to need planning permission (see chapter 15). However, if you occupy rented or leasehold property check that there are no restrictions on business use.

It is not necessary to register a sole trader business in any way, although you will need to declare yourself for VAT to HM Customs within 30 days if your turnover (sales) is likely to be over £21,300 in 12 months, or over £7,250 in any quarter.

For personal tax purposes you will be assessed under Schedule D. As a sole trader you will be taxed on the whole of your taxable profits, regardless of whether you have 'drawn' all these profits as personal income. You may think this a disadvantage compared with a limited liability company where much of the business' profits are untaxed. Your local tax office will probably be prepared to wait until six months after you have started trading before it wants income to be declared, although you should notify the Inspector of Taxes of your circumstances immediately. Tax under Schedule D is collected in two half-yearly payments.

You will have to make National Insurance contributions under Class 2 and Class 4 – the latter being profits related. Obtain details from your local Social Security office and decide whether you are going to make payments through direct debit or by stamping your card weekly with National Insurance stamps from a Post Office. It is sometimes possible to delay payments under Class 2 and 4 for one year.

The 1981 Companies Act abolished the Registrar of Business Names, so it is no longer necessary to register the name of your business. But you must display the proprietor's name on the business premises and on any correspondence. You must also check that your business name cannot be confused with that of any other business. Court action can result from any confusion of this kind. The Department of Trade & Industry can help if you are in doubt.

The main disadvantage of being a sole trader is that, in the eyes of the law, you and your business are the same entity. This means that in the event of bankruptcy your personal assets can be called upon to pay off creditors. Broadly speaking you should not set up a sole tradership if your business is going to depend on just a handful of customers who will insist on lengthy credit periods before they pay you. This is how businesses run out of cash and go bust. If you are a sole trader in a cash business, such as running a shop or a restaurant, where money is paid to you on the spot you are less exposed to financial disaster.

A definite advantage of being a sole trader is that Schedule D offers far greater scope for tax planning. When you are running a business from home there is allowance for charging expenses incurred in the running of the business, like lighting, heat, telephone and rates, against tax. There is also the opportunity to relieve any losses made in a business' first four years by setting them against your income of the three preceding years. It is also possible to carry forward relief against losses to be set against the profits of future years. These provisions can be a much-needed boost to cash flow in the early years of a business, particularly to someone who has given up a high wage job. These repayments usually also carry a tax-free repayment bonus which makes them even more attractive. But the trade concerned must from the beginning have been carried out with a 'reasonable' expectation of making profits in a 'reasonable' amount of time.

Partnerships

As in a sole tradership, the same problem of unlimited liability for business debts applies to partnerships. It is possible to get around this problem for one or more of the partners by making someone a salaried partner rather than a profit-sharing partner. This can be useful when someone's personal tax and financial circumstances make it difficult for them to become a full 'equity' partner.

The important thing in a partnership is to draw up a partnership agreement. Many partnerships fail to do this – at their peril. There are no strict regulations about partnership agreements, although there is a rough model for these arrangements in the 1890 Partnership Act. The sort of issues which should be addressed in a partnership agreement include:

- The sharing of profits and losses and the amount of capital which should be contributed by each partner and how it might be withdrawn.
- How long the partnership is to last and under what circumstances and conditions new partners can be admitted.
  If a partnership is allowed to run for ever, there can be problems in expelling a partner.
- The voting structure you require. Equal voting rights may not be appropriate particularly if you are the founding partner and want to always be in a controlling situation.
- How assets will be distributed if the partnership breaks up or one partner retires or leaves.
- Who owns the business premises – the individuals or the partnership? On what basis is interest to be repaid?

Partnerships are also assessed under Schedule D for tax purposes, although the Inland Revenue regards the partnership as a single entity and each partner is liable for the total amount. In other words, if one partner could not pay his own share of the income tax for some reason, the other partner can be asked to make up the difference.

Reliefs are available against losses in the same way as for a sole trader and partners can choose individually how they wish to employ these reliefs. The losses will be apportioned in accordance with the profit-sharing ratio.

A partnership carries the obvious advantage of strengthening a business by the addition of extra skills and personal resources. It can also help reduce the feeling of isolation which can afflict many business self-starters and so keep morale high. But partnerships can, and do, go very wrong. People fall out, particularly if things go badly, and if there is no partnership agreement all sorts of litigation and bitter feelings can ensue. If you are going into partnership with someone you have never worked with before it may be a good idea to have a trial period – perhaps with one of you working on a salaried basis rather than as a full equity partner.

Limited liability

Many people will not contemplate setting up a limited liability company until their sole tradership or partnership has started to grow convincingly. But there may be exceptions depending on the type of business and its exposure to credit risk and trade debt. One of the major attractions of a limited liability company is that, as its name implies, its shareholders have a limited liability to the company's debt in the event of failure and can, in principal anyway, separate their personal financial affairs from those of the company.

The limited liability company is rarely everything it seems. Although you cannot be asked to repay creditors and financiers if the company fails (unless you have been found guilty of 'wrongful trading' under the 1986 Insolvency Act) as a director you will almost certainly have been asked by your bankers to put up personal assets to secure the company's borrowings. Some people think this makes a mockery of the limited liability concept but you will rarely find a small company director who has not put his house on the line for the sake of his or her business.

Giving your company the separate identity under the law which is obtained by limited liability, means that you will take on far more responsibilities and public duties than is the case with the relative anonymity of being a sole trader or partnership.

There is, for a start, a huge body of company legislation which can affect you. There are over 200 different ways in which a company director can break the law. Queries about the law can be addressed to the Registrar of Companies. You will also have to keep much more detailed books and pay for an auditor to perform the statutory annual checking of your figures which then have to filed at Companies House. Although there are simpler reporting requirements for the smaller limited liability company, it may come as a shock to you that your business is no longer a confidential affair between you, the accountant and the taxman.

Anyone can now know the details of your company's performance – including how much you are paying yourself. If you like secrecy, limited liability is probably not for you.

Other disadvantages of limited liability include:

- Sole traders or partnerships have more room to take advantage of trading losses which can be offset against prior year income. In a limited liability company tax must be paid on salaries or income received by directors in the normal PAYE manner.
- Directors in an incorporated business cannot withdraw or introduce cash into a business without tax implications. In an unincorporated business you are free to move cash around to your own convenience.
- Because a sole trader is usually assessed for tax on income arising in a period ending in the preceding tax year, tax falls due for payment in two instalments – one on 1st January, the other on 1st July. Incorporated businesses have to pay their corporation tax far sooner – nine months after the end of their accounting period – and therefore lose this considerable benefit to their cash flow.

Advantages of limited liability include:

- Enhanced business 'image' which may help sometimes in securing orders and general marketing.
- An incorporated business only pays corporation tax on profits retained in the business, whereas a sole trader pays tax on total profits. Thus, if your marginal income tax rate is higher than the marginal rate of corporation tax there might be tax advantages in becoming incorporated. At present the 'small companies' rate of corporation tax is 27% where taxable profit is below £100,000.
- In general it is possible to build up a pension more tax efficiently in an incorporated business.
- More funding opportunities are open to an incorporated business, including venture capital and special lending schemes, such as the Loan Guarantee Scheme.

Stages in forming an incorporated business.

- Find a company registration agent. They advertise in the national press and for £100-£200 will do most of the paperwork for you. It is often advisable to accept an 'off the shelf' company.

This is quicker and can have tax advantages if the company has a record of trading losses.

- Select a company name. The Department of Trade and Industry publishes a booklet 'Business Names – Guidance Notes' which gives some advice. Check at Companies House that no other business is using the same name.

- There are two principal documents which you must complete: 'Memorandum of Association' and 'Articles of Association'. Your accountant will provide you with technical help. The company needs two directors and they must both own at least one share each. The Memorandum details the amount and type of share capital put into the business. The Articles of Association set out the company's rules and most businesses choose to use the model set out in the Companies Act. The Articles also set out voting rights, so make sure you structure voting control in a way which suits you.

- Once you receive a Certificate of Incorporation from the Registrar of Companies, you can start trading.

3. Starting up

You have cross-examined yourself about your reasons for going it alone, assessed your strengths and weaknesses, weighed up the risks, and decided what form of business you are going to set up.

But don't plunge in yet. There is still much research to do, advice to obtain, planning to complete. At this stage you feel ready to make the commitment to start working for yourself, but you still need to seek advice and information. Most importantly, you need to make a full evaluation of your business idea and determine, as far as you possibly can, whether it stands a reasonable chance of succeeding.

Market research

It is amazing how little basic market research most business self-starters conduct. Even many large businesses are woefully poor at this essential part of business planning. So why not seize an immediate market advantage by just taking the trouble to spend a little time researching the market you propose to enter?

Suppose, for example, you want to set up as a window cleaning business in your local area. How many other window cleaners are operating in the same area? It is not difficult to find out. Go to your local library and consult business directories such as the Yellow Pages. As an alternative, knock on doors in the housing areas you propose to work and politely ask whether anyone is already cleaning their windows, have they been approached by more than one window cleaner, how often do they call, is the customer satisfied with the job, how much are they being charged etc.

Establish how many windows you could clean a day and divide the number of properties in an area by the number of window cleaners at work. Is there a gap in the market? Perhaps you could afford to undercut on prices in order to seize your market advantage. Consider whether you might go one better than the opposition and perhaps offer another service as well. How about combining window cleaning with drain clearing, or gardening?

Alternatively, you may be proposing to set up a small shop selling do-it-yourself equipment. The first step, clearly, is to see what other DIY retailers exist in the area. Then do some window shopping to see what ranges they are marketing and which ones are selling best. More importantly ask yourself what aren't they providing to the consumer – are there any gaps you might fill?

But you should go further. A little bit of research in libraries, trade bodies and the national press will provide details on the size of the DIY market in Britain; its growth rates after allowing for inflation, and the amount per head of population being spent on DIY goods.

Some simple arithmetic can then show you what level of spending per local inhabitant you might expect in your area and thus what level of income to budget for in your own shop. These are rough-and-ready calculations, but without them you are probably making over-optimistic assumptions on the back of an envelope, and thus living in a business fantasy land.

What are the strengths of my competitors?

You need to know as much as possible about your competitors. If nothing else, knowing how your competitors operate will tell you much about the fundamental workings of your own proposed business. But you have to do a little leg-work to discover all their procedures.

If your competitors are incorporated businesses go to Companies House and research their turnover and profits from their filed accounts. Divide their turnover into their profits and you have already found the 'profit-margin' of one of your competitors. Find out what your competitors are charging; are they offering discounts and how much; what credit terms do they offer to customers; how efficient are their delivery systems? And how good or indifferent are the products or services they offer? Only by knowing these details will you gain the information on which to base your own business strategy. Without them you are fighting in the dark.

A slogan for my business

It is highly unlikely that you are setting up a business offering a product or service which no-one has thought of before. Most businesses, successful ones at that, are 'me too' businesses which merely try to reproduce someone else's achievements.

There is nothing wrong with copying an idea like this, as long as you have had the inspiration to think up a Unique Selling Proposition (USP) which will differentiate your business from the others.

Think of a slogan to fit your marketing message and make sure you stick to it when operating your business. "The Cheapest in Town"; "Next Day Delivery at All Times"; "Quality comes First"; "We Sell Only the Best". Anything, in fact, which you believe will set your business aside from the competition – giving it the 'edge' in the marketplace which will be essential if it is to succeed.

Help from the Government

When you set up in business it is tempting to think that the Government is a weight on your back, tying you up with red tape and bureaucratic detail. In fact, central government can provide a wealth of basic advice and information for the business self-starter if you know where to go.

Full details on where to obtain guidance on a wide range of business matters can be found in the final chapter of this book. But for any problem which arises in the early stages of setting up and running your business, the Department of Trade & Industry's Small Firms Service (SFS) provides information and professional counselling of an extremely high standard.

Even if you are just thinking of starting your own business the SFS is the ideal first port of call for anyone seeking assistance. The SFS can provide advice on everything from raising money to marketing and premises, and it also provides guidance on other government aid schemes.

There are 12 Small Firms Centres distributed throughout the country, with over 80 Area Counselling Offices. To contact your regional Small Firms Centre, dial 100 and ask the operator for *Freefone Enterprise*.

Help from your accountant

There are good accountants and not such good ones. Ask around for a recommendation of who to use. In particular, find an accountant who specialises in small firms. The use of an accountant is discussed in greater detail in chapter 11, so it is sufficient to say here that the accountant is probably going to be your confidant in these early stages. To believe you don't need your accountant's advice is foolish. You can save yourself considerable time and money by joining forces with an accountant at an early stage and obtaining key advice on personal and company tax planning, corporate structure, budgeting and planning as well as general business practice.

Help from your bank

It is a wise entrepreneur who gets the bank manager on his or her side to start with. You will probably be surprised by how much money the banks are geared up to offer to those starting up in business. But what bank managers dislike more than anything about young businesses is the lack of information they provide about themselves. Make it a habit from the outset to keep in regular touch with your bank manager – send monthly reports, if possible – and don't be afraid to ask his advice on any problems which arise.

Banks produce a wealth of literature which can be very useful for small businesses. The banks also have many specialist departments which branch managers can call upon if their clients require detailed counselling. Make use of them. Your bank manager will be flattered if you look upon him and his bank as business experts. See chapter 5 for more details.

The financial consequences

Armed with advice from all quarters, and with a bank manager and an accountant on your side, you must be sure that when you take the plunge you are still going to be able to feed yourself. A typical mistake made by many business self-starters is that they underestimate the amount of time it takes to get a business running. It is foolhardy to abandon a full-time job or regular dole cheque without thoroughly planning your expected pattern of income.

Ideally, you will have been planning your business's launch-day through the latter weeks of your previous employment. This way you reduce the amount of money you will be drawing out of your business capital just to pay yourself, while you are still attending to all the detail of setting up. It can take six months and sometimes more to get a small business fully funded, equipped and ready to trade.

It is even worth considering whether you can begin your business on a part-time basis until you have built up sufficient earnings momentum to be confident of making the split from full-time employment.

If you are moving into self-employment from a position as an employee, you will have presumably built up a savings cushion which will pay your outgoings until your business is under way. Remember, it can take a few months to make that first sale, and up to another three months for the first payment to come in. Unless you have the resources, either borrowed or saved, to cover your own costs for at least six months then, in most businesses, you are likely to be in trouble before very long.

Coming off the dole

Moving away from the peace of mind of regular social security and unemployment benefit into the uncertainties of self-employment is a big step for anyone who is out of work. Indeed, without a lump-sum redundancy payoff or personal savings of some sort, the risk involved will usually be too great to contemplate.

Anyone who is unemployed and is thinking of self-employment is best advised to spend many months in preparation – researching and planning his or her idea and discussing the plan with experts and at business advice centres. Remember, that when you start up as a sole trader, you must register under Schedule D for tax purposes and start making Class 2 National Insurance contributions. All social security and unemployment benefit will usually cease immediately.

It is sometimes possible to delay National Insurance contributions for one year and, as mentioned earlier, the tax inspector will let you trade for six months before he wants a declaration of income. As discussed in chapter 2 you may also be able to receive tax repayments on income from previous employment, by setting them against any early losses you make.

On the other hand it will be far more difficult to return to the full social security and unemployment benefits that you were receiving, should you decide your business is not working and you want to rejoin the dole queue. You may be able to claim supplementary benefits but not earnings-related pensions, widow's benefit or those benefits for industrial injury.

The Enterprise Allowance Scheme

Unemployed people who want to start their own business and don't want to lose all their unemployment benefits can take advantage of a limited number of places on the government's Enterprise Allowance Scheme. Under the EAS, the Manpower

Services Commission (MSC) will pay you £40 per week for one year to supplement income from your business.

Your local Job Centre will explain the full details of the scheme and will also put you in touch with a counsellor from the government's Small Firms Service who will help to develop your basic idea.

There are restrictions on the EAS which will make it unsuitable for some people. You must, for a start, be able to prove that you have £1,000 to put into the proposed business or are able to raise that amount through overdraft. You must also have been out of work for at least 8 weeks before you receive the benefit and the MSC must approve the proposed business.

The business must be small (employing no more than 20 people) and it must be totally new – i.e. it does not apply when you are taking over an existing business.

Help with tourism businesses

The government has singled out tourism as one sector where entrepreneurs should receive extra-special help. Assistance can be provided towards the cost of projects like hotel improvements, amenities and visitor attractions. In Wales help is given for projects involving as little as £5,000 or less, which are aimed at raising the standard of resort accommodation.

Contact your national tourist board or one of the 12 regional tourist boards in England.

4. Planning ahead

Good planning is at the heart of any successful business venture.
Even though it may sound no more than common sense to plan
your business carefully, you would be surprised how few companies
– sometimes even quite large and experienced ones – are
well-practised in this area. Planning in business is not something
which should be restricted to sizeable incorporated firms with
complicated budgets. The sole trader setting up in his garage and
proposing to achieve sales of only £15,000 in his first year should be
as alert to the benefits of planning as the executive of a big
multi-national corporation. The principles of business planning are
the same regardless of the size of the company.

Preparing the business plan

Every type of business, new or already running, should have a
business plan. This is not a one-off document prepared when raising
finance or at the beginning of each year, only to be then put in a
drawer and forgotten. The business plan is your working brief, a
tool to assist management and sales, a constant reference against
which you check performance and obtain early warning of things
going wrong.

The basic elements of a business plan are:
- A plan for the proposed progress of the business, possibly
  stretching forward as far as five years.
- A model against which management can monitor and control the
  financial progress of the business.
- A thorough description of the business, its products or services,
  market background, finances and management, which can be
  used by banks and other financiers or advisers to assess its
  viability or progress.

Putting together a business plan is often the 'crunch' moment for
many would-be entrepreneurs. Ideas which sound fine when
discussed casually with friends can quickly look ill-judged once you
write them down on paper and see what happens when you start
refining assumptions, witnessing the effect of different selling
prices or of increasing raw material costs.

It is advisable to draw up two business plans; a two or three page summary, and the full-length version which can often be 25 pages or more. The point of the summary is that prospective financiers for your business do not want to wade through a large tome to gain a quick impression of the basic proposition. If they are interested they will ask to see the full plan, which is the one that should be your own working guide to the company.

You should not believe that the business plan is some magic formula to ensure future success. It is, indeed, no substitute for natural business ability and flair. Certainly, be prepared for what happens in reality to be different from what is in the business plan.

The virtue of having the plan, however, is that it permits you to detect divergences from the desired course and provides a flow of information on which you can take corrective action before it is too late.

The business plan should cover the following areas:

- A summary of the business. Briefly mention the essential elements of your plan.
- The business proposal. The basic idea, any history of the business so far and projections for the future.
- The management. Descriptions of yourself and any partners, details of careers, special skills and qualifications and proposed responsibilities in the business.
- Organisation. How will the business be controlled and monitored? How will performance be checked against budget?
- The product or service. Details of what you will be selling and why you believe it has a competitive edge.
- The market. A detailed assessment of the market you will be entering. Mention competitors, their market shares, sales, profits and prices.
- Sales strategy. How you will go about marketing your product or service and organise distribution and promotion.
- Operational strategy. How you will organise production runs, stocking and raw material purchases, sourcing and packing.
- Financial details. How much capital you are putting into the business, budgets and cash flow forecasts for the next three years.
- Sensitivity analysis. How your projections and cash flow would vary with changes in costs, prices and other imponderables.

- Financing requirements. How much do you need to raise to achieve proposed cash flows. Detail how you would be able to repay loans.

Watch the cash, not the profits

An important consideration when planning your business is to remember that profit is not the same as cash in the bank. There is probably no bigger reason why firms go bust than confusing profits and cash. Profit is a theoretical amount that you know you should have made on a certain transaction or in a given period. Cash is how much money you have sitting in the bank.

Suppose you sell a product for £100 and you calculate that the total cost to produce it – including raw materials, labour, rent, rates etc. – is £85. You have made a profit of £15 and think you are doing well.

But suppose your customer has not paid the £100 on time and you have already had to meet your raw material, labour, rent and other costs? This means you are showing a cash 'outflow' of £85 and, as far as your bank manager is concerned, you are £85 poorer.

This is the difference between profit and cash, and is why budgets and cash flow forecasts are so essential. Unless you know when money is likely to be flowing in and out of your business, you can very easily find yourself with bills mounting up and no cash in the bank to pay them – even though you are owed money by a string of customers. Technically you may be insolvent.

Budgets

The first financial plans you should produce are a sales and gross profit budget and an overheads budget. These will provide a forecast of the level of sales you hope to achieve in an annual or six-monthly period, set against the costs involved in producing them, including fixed costs.

Budgets should be realistic. Many businesses do not make profits in the first or even second years. It is no good constructing a budget just because it 'looks good' and shows the company making profits when, in reality, it is overstating its likely sales levels or understating costs, or both.

So the budget should always be drawn up by the person with the deepest understanding of the business – usually the founder or senior partner in the case of small firms.

To project sales is extremely difficult in a start-up business. This is where your market research should come in useful in allowing you to at least make a reasoned guess at what sort of market penetration you might expect to achieve. You will also need to have details on your pricing levels, on any anticipated changes in the market or any seasonal factors like the Christmas boom in the high street which may affect sales.

Don't forget to build in any price increases which you might put through, and consider the likely level of inflation during the year.

Determining the cost of your sales is no less difficult. You must separate those costs which vary with the sales level, from those fixed costs which we describe as 'overheads'. Cost of sales could include labour costs if your staffing is going to vary with orders. It will certainly include raw materials, postage and packing as well as things like energy consumption and general services.

Overheads are easier to establish because things like rent, rates and some labour costs are fixed and don't vary with sales, even though there can be many expenses involved in the setting up of a business – legal fees, office equipment etc. – which are unforeseen at the outset.

The profit made on sales against sales-related costs is known as 'gross profit'. A business's fixed overheads must be paid out of the gross profits achieved on sales. So the total costs for a business are its sales-related costs plus overheads.

The trick for anyone drawing up a budget is to determine what level of costs are advisable given the projected volume of sales and the gross profit achieved on them. Even if a certain level of losses is expected, it is not until a realistic sales budget is prepared that you can see whether you will be able to afford that office computer, new furniture, extra employees etc.

A sales and gross profit budget could look like this:

XYZ Ltd Sales and Gross Profit for year to 31.12.87 (£)							
1st quarter							
January		February		March		Total	
Sales	Profit	Sales	Profit	Sales	Profit	Sales	Profit
6,000	600	6,000	800	20,000	2,000	32,000	3,400

The important thing to realise about a simple statement of forecast profit and loss like this, is that it only projects expected sales invoiced in a particular period against the cost of those sales in the same interval. It does not mean that this money has actually been received during that time, or that money has gone out of the business to pay bills to the amount which is the difference between sales and profit.

A simplified overheads budget (which details fixed costs) might itemise the following:

XYZ Ltd Overheads Budget for year to 31.12.87 (£)	
1st quarter	
Overhead	Estimate
Rent	
Rates	
Insurance	
Heating and Lighting	
Telephone	
Stationery	
Loan servicing	
Accountancy/legal fees	
Other	_____
TOTAL	_____
Cash flow forecasting	

The sales and gross profit budget details show just how much your business is going to make or lose in any period before deducting central overheads. The cash flow forecast shows how the money relating to that budget plus the overheads budget is expected to move around during the year and what kind of cash balance the business is likely to have at the end of every month. This is a business's most important piece of financial planning. Until a cash flow projection is completed a business cannot know when it might go into the red during a year and by how much. Until it knows its likely cash position it will not know what kind of borrowing facility it might require from the bank. It will also be unable to plan confidently for either fixed asset expenditure on things like plant and equipment, or for the cost of building up stocks.

Unless you are in a cash business, such as retailing, a company may have to wait up to three months and longer to be paid for its goods or services. But a business has far less flexibility when it comes to paying fixed overheads and even sales-related costs like raw materials and delivery. The anticipation of these expected financial demands on a business makes up the cash flow projection.

Don't worry if your cash flow projections seem to be very inaccurate at first – they usually are. The more experience you gain, the more you will be able to judge future expenditure and income, and fine tune your cash flow forecasts.

In the example shown on the opposite page, it can be seen that XYZ Ltd. does not receive any money for goods supplied until April and that its cash position deteriorates until the end of May where the cash situation was negative by £77,600. In other words this business, apart from the £30,000 of start-up capital which it began with, would have required bank or other facilities of £77,600 to meet all its debts.

It will be obvious that by varying sales levels, prices and costs you can perform a sensitivity analysis on such a cash projection and thereby determine what effects such changes would have on the cash situation. This would enable you to construct a 'best' and 'worst' case cash flow and, again, permit you a clearer picture of what financial requirements you will need in the beginning.

Although this cash flow forecast is for an incorporated business it applies equally to a sole trader or partnership.

Breakeven point

A vital figure you must keep in mind all the time is your business's breakeven point. This is defined as the level of sales you must achieve in a set period to cover all costs. In other words, if your monthly budget shows that your costs are £2,000 per month, you need to sell goods to the value of £2,000 to break even. This may sound like a very simple point, but in the confusion of invoices and deliveries which deluge the typical business it is very easy to forget what your breakeven point is, and by doing so it is easy to begin to lose sight of how your business is performing.

If you are failing to achieve breakeven point you know that you must start reducing your cost of sales and thus lower the breakeven point. This is essential business planning and applied rigorously can save many a business from an early death.

A specimen simplified cash flow forecast may look like this:

XYZ Ltd Cash Flow Forecast for year ending 31.12.87 (£)						
	Jan.	Feb.	March	April	May	June
CASH IN						
Capital injected	30,000	–	–	–	–	–
Sales received	0	0	0	6,000	8,000	25,000
–	30,000	0	0	6,000	8,000	25,000
CASH OUT						
Raw materials	10,000	12,000	8,000	7,000	9,000	10,000
Salaries	3,000	3,000	3,000	3,000	3,000	3,000
Rents and rates	6,000	6,000	6,000	6,000	6,000	6,000
Promotion	2,500	2,000	1,000	1,000	2,000	2,000
Transport	500	800	800	1,000	1,000	1,500
Fixed assets	18,000	–	–	–	–	–
–	40,000	23,800	18,800	18,000	21,000	22,500
CASH BALANCE						
At end month	(10,000)	(23,800)	(18,800)	(12,000)	(13,000)	2,500
Brought forward	0	(10,000)	(33,800)	(52,600)	(64,600)	(77,600)
NET CASH BALANCE	(10,000)	(33,800)	(52,600)	(64,600)	(77,600)	(75,100)

Profit margins

You often hear business people talk about profit margins. This is the percentage return which your selling price represents on the total cost of production. If you sell something for £100 which has cost £80 to produce, your profit margin is 20%. This not only shows how 'profitable' your business has become, but it is also a measure of comparison with the performance of competing companies.

Another important ratio is the gross profit margin which is the same as above but includes only the variable costs – materials, labour, delivery – which change relative to the amount of sales activity in a business. Because this figure excludes the direct costs, like rent and rates, it will be a higher percentage than a normal profit margin, but it is a better guide to how income is being generated by a given level of sales. If the business was operating below breakeven point, the gross profit margin is only making a contribution to direct costs. Above breakeven point, the gross profit margin is a good indicator of the earning power of the company.

It is worth familiarising yourself with the breakeven and profit margin concepts. Apart from impressing the bank manager with your knowledge of the most important concepts in business, they are invaluable day-to-day guides which enable you to keep a constant mental picture of how your business is progressing.

Summary of key points

Business plan	=	Summary of business strategy, budgets, cash projections and financial requirements.
Cost of sales	=	Variable costs like raw materials, labour and delivery which change with level of sales.
Overheads	=	Fixed costs like rent and rates which do not change with level of sales.
Gross profit	=	Sales figure after deduction of cost of sales.
Sales and gross profit budget	=	Forecast of expected sales and gross profit.
Cash flow	=	Flow of cash in and out of the business account.
Breakeven point	=	The level of sales needed to cover all costs.

$$\text{Profit margin (\%)} = \frac{\text{Sales} - (\text{Overheads} + \text{Cost of sales})}{\text{Sales}}$$

$$\text{Gross profit margin} = \frac{\text{Sales} - \text{Cost of sales}}{\text{Sales}}$$

5. Raising finance

There is probably more anguish over raising finance than any other part of a small business's operation. Whether you are starting out as a sole trader on Schedule D or as an incorporated company, be prepared to discover that gulf which always seems to separate the entrepreneur and the financier.

It is a pity that this gulf still exists in Britain despite the attempts, in recent years, of bankers,, venture capitalists and, to some extent, the government to forge more of a partnership with young businesses. In truth, the misunderstandings which arise in this area owe a lot to both parties. The financiers are often poorly equipped to judge some business plans and are too often only prepared to make funds available on the most punishing terms. Entrepreneurs are equally often ill-prepared and arrogant when they go to raise finance.

The basic rules about getting the money you need to get started are really very simple. Stick to them and you will find that the bankers' boast of 'plenty of money available' is actually not very far from the truth.

Looking at you

Any provider of funds for business will say that the most important factor to them in judging a business proposition is the person or persons who have come to them for money. In other words, *you*.

It is important to realise that this is no idle, rather obvious remark by the financiers. They mean it. Always remember that it is someone else's money which is going to be invested in your business. Whoever is the purveyor of that money wants a good idea of whether he is going to get that money back. Ultimately it can only be based on a judgement of you – your character, record, experience, intelligence and honesty – that a decision to invest can be made.

This personal test is the point at which most business self-starters fail in raising funds. After all, if there is something wrong with your business plan, market research, cash flows or budget projections, then any good bank manager or other financier can point those out and advise you to go away, do some more homework, and come back later. But if you make a bad personal impression at that first meeting it might take a great deal to overcome it later.

Take the true case of the man who wanted to start his own off-licence. His idea of explaining his plans was to slam down a crate of samples on the bank manager's desk. Needless to say, the bank manager was not impressed.

So don't ruin your chances right from the start by being arrogant, defensive and badly prepared. Don't go and see your bank manager without a business plan and don't expect him or her to be well briefed in the market you are proposing to enter. Be particularly mindful that the bank manager will be most interested in your cash flow forecast because that is what will indicate whether the bank stands a chance of getting its money repaid.

Show your bank manager that you are confident, but also humble. The bank is likely to be more impressed if you are eager for advice and comment than if you immediately get yourself into a corner defending your plans and projections. The bank manager will probably have seen hundreds of business plans like yours and his or her opinion should be viewed as valuable assistance. If the bank sees that you are the sort of person who can take advice, it will have evidence of your intelligence. You are already half way there.

Approaching the bank

Whether you are setting up as a sole trader, partnership or an incorporated company, the bank will want to see the following:

- Business plans, as discussed in chapter 4, which must include budget and cash flow projections.
- Details of how much you are personally prepared to put into the business.
- Evidence that you have sufficient security (i.e. personal property) to act as collateral on the loan.
- Details of how you will repay the loan, if not already described in cash flow forecast.

For your first meeting with the bank it may not be necessary to produce the full scale business plan – the shorter two/three page version will often suffice, as long as there is an abbreviated cash flow forecast. If the bank manager seems interested you can impress him/her further by producing the fuller document.

The big shock for many self-starters in business is the way lenders always insist on full security for their loans, which they can call up should you be unable to repay. For most people this involves putting up their homes as security. Cruel as this often seems, there is little point complaining. It is one of those facts of life. If you don't own your own home, or don't have any other personal security such as a car, valuables or perhaps an investment policy then you are unlikely to receive much sympathy, or money, from a bank.

But don't be put off because you get a bad reception at one particular bank. Shop around and go to different banks, including some of the overseas banks which have come to Britain in recent years. You will find that bank policies can differ greatly when it comes to lending to small businesses, and so do the branch managers and regional specialists to whom you will be talking. Also, keep your accountant informed about your talks with bankers and think about taking him along with you when meeting the bank manager.

Overdrafts

The type of finance which is best for you will depend on the type of business you are setting up, the amount required and for what purpose.

Most people going into one-person self-employment will rarely require anything other than the normal overdraft facility. The good thing about overdraft facilities is that, unlike a loan, you only pay interest on the amount by which you are overdrawn. The overdraft is thus particularly useful to businesses which have a seasonal pattern and can be short of cash at some times of the year and relatively well-off at others.

Interest on overdrafts is usually 2–3% above base rates and, of course, varies as the base rate fluctuates. This means you must calculate in your cash flows the effects of higher interest rates on your ability to service the overdraft. Overdrafts can be for quite large amounts so don't make the frequent mistake of underestimating your cash requirements when going to the bank. Ask for a little more than you really think you will need, just in case. Remember, every time you go to the bank for a higher overdraft, additional arrangement fees are applied.

On the other hand, don't overestimate your cash requirements. Many people setting up shops or other retail businesses start off by ordering vast amounts of stock only to find that sales don't progress as anticipated and that they have tied up capital in an inefficient way. The amount of stock you order will depend on how many times a year that stock is sold, or 'turned over'. If your business is going to turn over its stock 12 times a year and you start out by ordering three months' worth of stock you are almost certainly wasting money.

Loans

Businesses looking for large sums to finance assets like premises and equipment will find overdraft facilities unsuitable. Because these assets need to be financed over a longer period, the relative certainty of a loan is required.

A loan can carry a fixed repayment period for up to 20 years, although it is difficult to get banks to agree on anything longer than 10 years. Today, banks offer a variety of special loan schemes to help small businesses and the terms they carry can be quite flexible, so it is worth comparing different arrangements. As with overdrafts, the borrower pays a few per cent over base rate, although it is now possible to take out fixed rate loans and sometimes switch to a fluctuating rate loan later. The opposite is also true in some cases, where you can start out at a variable rate and switch to a fixed rate later.

Even if you are a one-man band business it is sometimes worth trying to persuade your bank manager to consider offering you a loan rather than the ubiquitous overdraft. Basically, banks prefer to lend on overdraft, while businesses like the greater certainty of a loan.

Banks won't make business loans below £15,000, but even the smallest of concerns might need capital items like vehicles or office equipment. If your business plan is up to scratch you might be able to persuade your bank to make you the type of loan it would normally reserve for a larger enterprise. And if one bank won't go along with that – go and ask another.

Banks have many fancy names for their loan schemes but, in reality, they all come down to a negotiated agreement between the bank and you. Think flexibly because the bank will certainly vary the conditions to suit itself. On some loans, for example, you might be able to negotiate a 'capital holiday' repayment period, where you don't have to repay any of the capital for the first year or so.

These days banks are highly conscious of the more competitive air that has emerged in high street lending. The 'threat' of taking your proposal to the bank across the road might well have the desired effect.

The Government's Loan Guarantee Scheme

Since 1981 the Government has endeavoured to ease the problems of funding small firms through its Loan Guarantee Scheme. The aim of the LGS is to prevent good business ideas from failing through lack of personal security, by backing loans made by banks. So far it has had varying degrees of success, but the LGS is now well established and by 1987 had helped more than 15,000 firms.

The LGS is available through banks to sole traders, partnerships, co-operatives and limited companies. The loan, which has no lower limit but goes up to £75,000, can be for working capital (to pay wages, running costs etc), fixed capital or project development costs (professional advice, research etc).

The loan is made by a bank but the Government guarantees 70% of the outstanding amount. So if your business fails the Government will pay the bank 70% of the money. The bank is not allowed to ask for personal security from the lender, although it can ask for business assets (like stock or property) to be pledged as security on the outstanding 30% of the loan.

Loans under the LGS are medium term – two to seven years – and sometimes capital holiday repayment periods can be negotiated. The bank charges interest on the loan in the normal way and the government also charges a 2½% per annum premium on the 70% of the oustanding balance of the loan. This adds 1.75% per annum to the cost of the loan. This makes the LGS an expensive form of borrowing but it has obvious attractions for entrepreneurs who would normally be unable to raise a loan from the bank.

A bank will ask just the same questions about an LGS proposal as it would about any other business plan. But the bank is not required to award an LGS loan if you would otherwise be able to secure a loan through normal routes.

Banks have tended to vary in their enthusiasm for the LGS, although today practically all the high street banks operate the scheme and understand its workings. Basically, you should not go for an LGS loan unless it is absolutely necessary. It is expensive, particularly if interest rates are on the way up. it also has less flexibility than an overdraft because the loan must be taken either in one lump or in no more than four stages over the first two years.

Details about the scheme are available from any bank or you can contact:

Department of Employment, Loan Guarantee Unit,
Room 221, Steel House,
11 Tothill Street,
London SW1H 9NF.
Tel: 01-213 3858/5358

Venture capital

Larger incorporated businesses, whether start-ups or with a track record, frequently find that loans are too much of a burden to carry before a growth momentum has been established. The alternative is equity funding, where the financiers provide money in return for a stake in the share capital of the company. When equity finance like this is provided to young, high risk companies it is referred to as 'venture capital'.

Venture capital is not for sole traders or partnerships. If you are simply becoming self-employed or teaming up with others in an unincorporated business, your routes to finance will be mostly restricted to overdraft and loan financing.

The advantage of venture capital to a company is that you receive money in a lump sum without the need to repay it or, in most cases, even pay a dividend on the shares which have been taken up by the investor. This is risk investment in its purest form and in Britain today there is a growing amount of such money available to back good business propositions. What the investor of venture capital is seeking is to make a capital windfall by selling his shares in, say, five years' time for a large profit. In other words, the venture capitalist will be expecting your company either to become a quoted company – perhaps on the Unlisted Securities Market – or be taken over by another company so that he has the opportunity to sell his shares. Only certain types of proposition with top-notch management and the potential for high growth will qualify for this type of financing.

Most people starting off in business in a small way typically seek capital in the £10,000–50,000 region. Regrettably, this is not the sort of funding which can normally attract venture capital finance. Venture capitalists, with perhaps a few exceptions, will only start to get interested if something in excess of £100,000 is required.

If you are running, or intend to run, an incorporated business seeking this level of finance, it is important to understand that you are surrendering part of the control of your business in return for finance. For very young companies, particularly start-ups, it may be that the venture capitalist will want as much as 40% of your business and will expect to have his own person on your board and demand regular reports and management accounts. The venture capitalist can also have a large say in the future ownership of your business, since he will be looking for his 'out' when he realises his investment and takes a profit.

In recent years there has been a tendency for the equity-financing of companies to concentrate on the later-stage companies requiring so-called 'development capital'. Obtaining venture capital for 'green field', start-up projects is not easy. If you are setting up an incorporated business and are interested in the possibility of attracting venture capital, your best advice is to talk to your accountant or bank manager. Alternatively, consult Britain's largest venture and development capital group Investors in Industry plc (3i) at 91 Waterloo Road, London, SE1 8XP. 3i will make venture capital available to start-ups, sometimes with loan money as well, on possibly a less demanding assessment than other independent venture capital groups. Regard 3i as a kind of sieve. If your application for venture capital financing does not get through 3i, it probably won't be accepted by anyone else.

If you want to pursue equity financing further, a fuller list of venture capitalists can be obtained through:

The British Venture Capital Association,
1 Surrey Street,
London WC2R 2PS.
Tel: 01-836 5702

Business Expansion Scheme

Incorporated businesses who have been unsuccessful in raising venture capital through 3i or any of the other big funds can consider the Business Expansion Scheme. The BES is a government-supported equity financing scheme. It is designed to encourage private individuals to support small firms by purchasing shares in those companies, in return for top rate marginal tax relief on their investments. An investor can put up to £40,000 a year into a business but must keep his or her investment in the business for a minimum of five years to claim all the tax relief. On an investment of £10,000 the benefit to a taxpayer on 60% rate tax would be £6,000.

Any local investors with money of this sort to spare are worth talking to about your proposition. Your own family are excluded from BES investments in your business. Today most BES money is invested indirectly through large BES funds, but like most venture capital groups these funds are usually only concerned with six-figure deals.

To obtain details of interested investors you should talk to your accountant, local enterprise agency or contact:

Electra Risk Capital,
65 Kingsway,
London WC2 6QT.
Tel: 01-831 6464

Electra keep a list of people keen on making BES investments.

Other sources of finance

It pays to be imaginative when trying to raise finance. Most self-starters think no further than their local bank, but there are many other sources of finance. Building societies are starting to dabble in the area of providing money for small companies and could soon become serious competition for the banks. It is also possible to raise money on the strength of a private pension policy, depending on your level of premiums and how long you have been making contributions. Local authorities, New Town bodies, urban development groups and enterprise agencies frequently run little-known schemes to help small companies get off the ground.

For local guidance try your accountant or, alternatively, the government Small Firms Service. Tel: *Freefone Enterprise*.

6. What should you charge?

Deciding how much to charge for your product or service may appear to be one of the easier decisions to take when setting up a business. In fact, pricing can be complicated and to get it wrong can, and very often does, put a new business in trouble right from the beginning.

It might seem that to arrive at a reasonable selling price you merely add up all your costs of production and add a fixed percentage, which gives you an adequate profit. Obviously you would keep an eye on the competition and try to undercut them on price if that was going to be your marketing strategy, or charge a premium if your product or service was that extra bit special.

The first thing that is wrong with a simple 'cost plus' approach to pricing like this is that it ignores the particular area in which you intend to operate. Some sectors have less room for price differentials than others. The retail trade, for example, has 'recommended' prices which come with the goods from the manufacturer. It will be very difficcult for you to charge even fractionally more than a competitor and get away with it. Equally, most retailers have similar basic costs and there will be little room for you to trim your rent, electricity, heating and other bills in order to charge lower prices.

In other fields the cost plus method could leave you charging too little for your product or service and thereby raising your breakeven point (see chapter 4) too high. Under-pricing is a typical error made by self-starters in business.

The truth is that the customer will ultimately determine what you can charge, and it is best to start out with some understanding of the laws of supply and demand which govern all markets.

How unique is my product or service?

It is easy for any entrepreneur to believe that his or her product or service is so good that it leaves the competition standing. If this really is the case and customers *are* unable to find anything similar on the market, then you can charge a high price. If you are in a 'me too' business, offering broadly the same that exists elsewhere in the market, you have limited room to ask premium prices.

The law of supply and demand says that if the price of something rises too high, demand will fall. At the same time, however, if you reduce the price too far, demand will also start to fall, as people begin to suspect poor quality. If you plotted this link between sales volume and prices you would get what is called a 'price-demand curve'. A price-demand curve always looks something like the one below, although every product or service will have its own particular shape. The degree to which sales volume changes with price is known as 'price elasticity'.

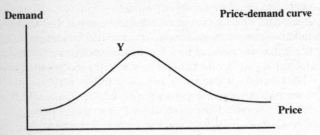

You should get to know the price elasticity of your product or service as soon as possible. This can be done by looking at competitors' prices, doing some market research, or even through a process of trial-and-error price adjustment in your own business.

The idea is to arrive at the highest possible selling price without killing demand. So, on the diagram, point Y is where you could expect to increase prices before seeing demand decline. It is important to look at the steepness of the curve (i.e. the decline in demand) beyond point Y. If you increased prices by 5% beyond point Y, does the curve drop away more than 5%? If it does, then although you will be getting more for what you do sell, your volume will drop too far, resulting in a lower sales figure.

Clearly, the ideal is to have a very shallow curve before point Y so that price increases manage to keep sales stable, even though volume demand is falling.

It can be seen that the cost-plus method of pricing is folly and that to match your prices to the market you need to be mindful of the laws of supply and demand and price elasticity. This means that when you are establishing the cost structure of your business you *must* begin with selling prices and work backwards. It is no good establishing a cost base first and then trying to achieve a selling price which covers all those costs and leaves some extra for profit.

Establishing your sales price

We saw in chapter 4 that the costs of a business are made up of its fixed costs, or overheads, and its sales-related costs. The problem of setting a price for the first time is that you don't know how much you are going to sell and so you cannot accurately forecast the sales-related or 'cost of sale' costs.

Suppose, for example, you are setting up a small manufacturing business producing wooden dolls. Your overheads – rent, rates etc – are, say, £10,000 per quarter. You anticipate that you will sell 2,000 dolls during this period and that the cost of manufacturing them will be £2 each.

So your total costs for the quarter will be:

Overheads	£10,000
Cost of sales	£ 4,000
Total costs	£14,000

In order to break even it is obvious that you must achieve an income of £14,000 which can only be reached if you have a selling price of £7 per doll. If you can sell at anything above £7 you will be making a profit.

But suppose you don't sell 2,000 dolls? If you only sold 1,000, your income would be £7,000, leaving you with a loss of £7,000.

You could, of course, simply put up the price of the doll by 100% and charge £14, but this would depend on how elastic prices were in this particular market (see above). What you have to do is adjust your overheads and cost of sales until you can manufacture the right number of dolls to meet demand, while selling them at a price which will allow you to break even.

This can be written as a simple equation:

$$\text{Breakeven Point} = \frac{\text{Fixed costs}}{\text{Selling price} - \text{Unit sales cost}}$$

To illustrate this equation in practice, suppose you see that you are going to sell no more than 1,000 dolls per quarter and you don't believe it is possible to reduce your fixed costs. What would your

breakeven sales price have to be? This can be shown using the
simple arithmetic on the previous page.

$$0 = \frac{£10,000}{£12\,(\times 1,000) - £2\,(\times 1,000)}$$

You can see that to break even the dolls would have to be priced
at £12 each. As this figure excludes any profit, in reality you would
have to price the dolls even higher. This could only be achieved if
the market was elastic enough to absorb the price increase without
it affecting demand levels. If this was impossible you would know
that you must either get your fixed costs down – perhaps by moving
to cheaper premises – or somehow get your unit sales cost down –
perhaps by shopping around for cheaper raw materials.

Controlling costs

You can now begin to see why the control of fixed and variable
costs is essential to the profitability of any business. It is no good
loading yourself up with expensive overheads, such as fancy
premises in the best part of town, if you are not going to achieve a
volume of sales, on the prices the market will tolerate, that will
bring you to breakeven.

To keep fixed overheads down the most obvious saving can be
made on premises. It may be advisable to start your business
working from home, rather than build in a heavy fixed cost for
office or workshop space right from the beginning. Certainly if you
are only working part-time or freelance you should not be spending
much on premises or equipment, because you will not be able to
earn enough to cover the costs.

The idea should be to make the majority of your costs variable.
Thus, if you could hire or rent plant and equipment when you need it,
rather than buy it and have it idle for much of the time, you would
make a saving. Where profit margins are thin even small reductions in
overhead costs can produce dramatic increases in profits.

Another area where big savings can be made is in efficient
purchasing of raw material and supplies and in stock control. As a rule
people are not good at selling until they have become proficient at
buying. The key to efficient buying is to realise that there is a trade-
off between obtaining discounts for bulk ordering and the higher
cost of carrying larger amounts of stock. This higher cost comes

about because you have tied up money – possibly borrowed money attracting interest – for stock which may not move for many months. Did the the discount for ordering bulk outweigh the cost of carrying the stock? If it didn't, that's inefficient buying.

Paying for yourself

The biggest cost in most first-time business is labour, and usually that means yourself. How you cost yourself is up to you and depends on whether you intend drawing a regular income or accept that it will vary with the fortunes of the business. Opinions differ about whether labour should be treated as a fixed or variable, sales-related cost. If you are running a small firm whose payroll will vary with the workload, obviously part of the labour cost is variable and should be treated as such. But in a one-person business it is probably best to regard your labour as a fixed cost and treat it as an overhead.

If you are entering a one-person labouring or other service-type business, you can establish a fairly precise charging basis for your time depending on a mixture of market rates, how much you expect to earn and how much time-per-job will be required.

For example, if you are becoming a one-person landscape gardener expecting to earn a gross income of £250 per week, working a 40-hour week, your hourly rate is £250/40 = £6.25.

In costing any job you must add any materials, travel costs etc, which are involved and give the customer a fairly precise estimate of the hours needed to complete the work and how you have arrived at the cost which you are quoting.

Many service businesses, even very large professional groups, never bother to quote hourly charging rates before they embark upon a job. There is much to be said for improved customer relations if you detail your charging rates beforehand, but what is important is that you have a firm idea of these rates and that they figure in your business plan. It is too easy in a service business to begin work which will be unprofitable because you have both underpriced yourself and underestimated the amount of time the job involves.

What about profits?

Many people going into self-employment or running small companies never, surprisingly, have much intention of making large profits. Their ambition is simply to break even, pay themselves a living wage and enjoy their independence. This is partly why the vast majority of small firms don't grow.

But profit is not a dirty word. It is essential if business as a whole is to grow and essential to you, however small your business, if it is to have a chance of surviving in the long term.

Unless your business makes a surplus of income over all costs (fixed and variable, and including your own drawings) it is unlikely to get any larger. For a start, you need profits to replace old equipment or renovate office premises. You also need profits to launch new marketing or promotional activities to boost sales. And without profits you are likely to be continually living on borrowed money until lack of growth finally saps your ability to service the debt.

How much profit?

There are no hard rules about how much profit businesses should expect to make. It depends on the business and the relationship between costs, volume and prices. In some high margin businesses profits can come to be 50% or more of the sales figure. In others, a few per cent is the best that can be expected. The size of margin a business is making can only be judged relative to that business's future financing requirements. In other words, how much money does that type of business need to be ploughed back into it for satisfactory future growth to be established?

Another way to look at profits is to think of 'return on funds employed'. This is the percentage return which one year's profits represent on all the money put into the business in the first place – both your own capital and that of the bank or other financiers. If you got to a stage where you were achieving a 25% return on funds employed, you would be doing very nicely.

So in pricing, don't forget to build in a profit element. It could be tempting to forget about profits for the first year or two of a business but this would be a mistake. It is far more difficult to put prices up than cut them.

In many private businesses any extra profit which is made goes straight into the pockets of the proprietors. If this is how you want to run your business, so be it. But if you are looking to build up a growth business you will need to re-invest most of those profits in the operation itself – improving product quality, buying more modern equipment, hiring more staff etc. So think 'profit' from day one.

7. Advertising and marketing

Many, if not most, people who go into business on their own do so because the idea of manufacturing a certain product or providing a certain type of service has always appealed to them. Regrettably, few begin the other way around and launch into something because they have seen an unfulfilled need in the marketplace. However, if you were in the former category you wouldn't be alone. Britain has always been dominated by production-led business people who tend to make a product or set up a service first and then think about whether anyone needs it afterwards. Two out of three top businesses in Britain admit that they are bad at marketing.

Marketing is not just about selling. It embraces everything from getting quality right on the production line, researching your customer base, to advertising and promotion. To be a winner in business you must be market-led. That is, guided in everything you do by what the customer wants, not by what appeals to you as a good idea for a business. Basic market research was discussed in chapter 3. Here we will look at identifying customers and getting across your sales message.

Who are my customers, and where are they?

Assuming you have done your market research and established that a particular demand for your product or service probably exists, you should stop and ask yourself exactly who these customers are and where you are likely to find them.

Depending on the particular market, customers can vary by their age, sex, occupation, income, professional awareness and geographical location.

Try to group the potential customers of your product or service together. For example, suppose you want to set up a fashion shop selling quality clothes to young people of both sexes. You will need to find a fairly affluent town or city whose population is not dominated by elderly or retired people, that has a high level of employment amongst the young and shows evidence (provided by other retailers) that there is a demand for fashionable clothes.

Very often you will not be able to reach your customers directly, but will have to deal through a retailer, wholesaler, dealer, agent or middle-man. This means that your effective selling price is reduced, because someone between you and your customers is taking their 'cut'. But you should identify the right intermediate person in the same way as you should identify your customers. Is the retailer you want to deal through, for example, located in the right area with the customer profile you need?

If you are selling to industry, identify where the types of business which might buy your product or service are located. For example, if you are selling a product which has specialist uses for the computer and high technology industries, it would be a waste of effort to try and sell throughout the country with a scatter-gun marketing approach. It would be better to focus on areas like the Thames Valley, Cambridge and Scotland where there are concentrations of this type of industry.

Finding out about your market

There is far more information about businesses, consumers and markets than you might imagine. Most public libraries have a business reference section where business directories are kept which will break down companies into sectors and list their addresses and telephone numbers. A great deal of market research is also made public these days, so you should ask the librarian if anything has been published on your particular speciality.

Chambers of Commerce are good sources of local business knowledge and you can also try national trade associations for lists of members. Local authorities can also be of assistance in helping you to build up a profile of local business and population. And don't forget the Government's Small Firms Service (Tel: Dial 100 and ask for *Freefone Enterprise*) which lists help with marketing amongst its counselling specialities. If you need more specialist help contact:

Institute of Marketing,
Moor Hall,
Cookham,
Maidenhead, Berks SL6 9QH.
Tel: 06285 24922.

Reaching your customer – advertising

Having identified who and where your customers are, you now need to alert them to the existence of your product or service.

The obvious route may appear to be advertising, but this depends on what type of business you are running. If you manufacture specialist products that are only sold to a handful of companies, advertising is a waste of time. Personal sales visits to the buyers of the companies concerned is the only effective way of reaching your market. On the other hand, if you are selling directly to consumers you need to inform a much larger market in terms of actual customers, and some form of local or national advertising will probably be required.

It is very easy to waste money on advertising. Once you are in business a range of different media will try to sell you 'space' but you should be mindful of your target market and ask which particular media are going to reach that market.

Remember that different media each have their own reader or viewer profiles. Some newspapers have readers in lower income brackets than other papers, and some simply have far larger circulations. For example, if you were selling a product to young people in your local area you might be tempted to put an advertisement in the local paper. But not all local papers are popular with young people – the possible alternative of advertising on local radio may give you access to your target group.

If you are selling to a specific sector of industry or commerce it can be more effective to advertise in the relevant trade magazines. But wherever you do advertise it will pay to experiment and monitor the responses you get from different media. This is easy if you place 'coupon' advertisements where the reader has to cut out a reply coupon to ask for more information. And when you receive a trade enquiry, ask where the enquirer heard about your business.

A rule of thumb to gauge the cost effectiveness of advertising is to find out the number of readers, listeners or viewers of a particular media outlet and see how much it is costing you to reach one thousand of them. The cost-per-thousand figure is a standard ratio in advertising, but it is by no means the only rule. Remember, for a specialist product or service, it will probably be cheaper to reach a thousand readers by placing an advertisement in a national newspaper, than by placing the same advertisement in the trade press. But the level and quality of response gained from the trade paper will probably be superior, as that media offers the reader profile relevant to the product or service concerned.

Most small businesses will generate their own advertising copy and place advertisements themselves. But don't dismiss out of hand the idea of using an advertising agency. There are many small local advertising agencies and some just specialise in buying the media space or time and leave the creative side up to you or another agency. The various media are becoming more complex all the time, so the advice of an agency specialist can be useful. More information about agencies can be obtained from:

Institute of Practitioners in Advertising,
44 Belgrave Square,
London SW1.
Tel: 01-235 7020

Direct mail advertising

Used properly, direct mail can be a highly effective means of advertising. But this medium is not cheap, and getting it wrong can be a costly blunder. The problem with direct mail is that it involves so many different skills – copy-writing, research, design, printing and mailing. It is asking quite a lot for the first-timer in business to be adept at all of these. Employing a direct mail agency is worth contemplating, although you might have to pay over £200 per day for their services.

The first step is to make sure that your product or service is suitable for advertising through direct mail. In direct mail a 1% response rate is regarded as quite good. So you should determine the cost of reaching that 1% compared with other forms of advertising.

For example, say you mail 1,000 addresses at a cost of £300. If you received a 1% response that means the cost of reaching each customer has been

$$\frac{£300}{10} = £30$$

If you are selling a product or service with a unit cost of less than £30, this is probably an inefficient way of marketing yourself. You would probably be better off spending that £300 on a quarter-page coupon advertisement in your local newspaper or a trade magazine, thereby reaching a much larger audience.

The most important aspect of direct mailing is to get the right mailing list. Obviously the list should be specifically related to your target market. Direct mail agents can provide lists but you can of course construct your own, even though it may be time-consuming. As your business builds up you should be developing your own customer list in-house, although you will probably need to supplement this with names from trade registers etc.

If you are writing your own 'copy' for a mailshot here are a few key points:

- Make it simple and to the point. Don't waffle.
- Begin by describing the advantage of the product or service to the customer in a few words.
- Throughout the letter or brochure insist that what you are selling has been designed to help the customer and not you. Always talk about the customer and not yourself or your business.
- The letter or brochure should end up asking the reader to respond in some way. Make this simple and make use of Freepost or the Business Reply Service.
- Use the envelope to repeat your sales message.

Little need be said about printers except you should shop around for quotes; prices vary enormously, as does quality.

The Post Office is well geared up to help direct mail users today and you should enquire about the 'bulk rebate service' and 'incentives for first time users'. Also ask about Freepost and the Business Reply Service, so that your target customer will not have to go to the trouble of finding a stamp – a real stumbling block in gaining a postal response.

Ask for the Post Office's booklets on direct response advertising. Further guidance about direct mail and mailing lists should be made to:

British Direct Marketing Association Ltd,
1 New Oxford Street,
London WC1A 1NQ.
Tel: 01-242 2254

Other direct selling methods

Advertising and direct mail will not be relevant to all types of business. Alternative methods of direct selling include:

- Telephone selling where you, your sales 'reps', or an agency sales force try to interest customers over the phone.
- Poster advertising. Useful way of raising local awareness.

- Sales leaflets. Delivering leaflets to homes or businesses in your local area is effective and relatively cheap. Keep it simple, say what is unique about your product and make it easy for the consumer to make a response (telephone number, coupon etc).
- Personal visits to customers. This is most effective where you have a small customer base and face-to-face contact is important.
- Sales tours. Potential customers are visited by proprietor or sales force for brief presentations or demonstrations. Most effective when calling upon consumers in their homes.
- Open days. If you have a small manufacturing company why not invite potential customers to see your operation?
- Exhibitions. Though not cheap for very small companies, exhibitions can be an excellent way of meeting new customers. Take trouble with your stand and make sure it puts across your product simply and dramatically. Have order forms on hand and be prepared to do business.

Using directories and databanks

There is a growing trend, both nationally and locally, to help businesses in their marketing by publishing the details of their products or services in directories or listing the information on computer databases. Directories like the Yellow Pages or Kellys are well known. But you should enquire locally (ask your Chamber of Commerce or local Enterprise Agency or Business Club) to see if any other directories exist where you can be listed.

Using agents or distributors

Employing an agent to market your product may sound like taking the pain out of selling. It can certainly be a highly effective and cheap way of making sales. The agent will usually be paid only according to the sales he or she makes, and so does not represent a fixed cost to your business. But remember that agents sell other products too and few are ever going to sound as knowledgeable and convincing abour your product as you do.

Skilfully selected agents can take some of the leg-work out of marketing – often important in a small business where much of the proprietor's time is involved in the manufacturing of the product or provision of the service. Be sure to negotiate the agency commission at the outset and set down any minimum sales volume requirements.

If you have a product which has the potential for national sales you should think about using a distribution network. By giving the distributor a discount and allocating him a specified geographical area, he will be effectively taking the cost of carrying stock off you and also, hopefully, guaranteeing you a minimum level of sales.

Distributors also have the advantage that they lend credibility to a new company's product. It can be very difficult for a new firm to get accepted in the market, but a good distributor lends its own reputation to your product.

Marketing for retail businesses

Many first-time retailers are tempted to think that the very existence of their shop is all the advertising they need. Sadly, this is not the case. You should consider the following to enhance your marketing:

- Local press advertising, especially with special promotional offers.
- Local radio advertising. Very effective for high street businesses.
- Leaflet drops. House to house postings of leaflets detailing prices and product ranges.
- In-store 'point-of-sale' advertising – posters, display stands, mobiles, special price tickets, etc.

Promotion

Promotion differs from pure 'selling' in that some kind of special offer, gimmick or campaign is involved to give your product or service that extra push in the marketplace. This can be very important, if not critical, for a new business which will inevitably struggle to get some kind of sales momentum going.

Most promotional schemes are dreamt up by big companies and their highly-paid advertising agents. But all the techniques are applicable to small businesses and it should take little imagination to see how they can be deployed to your own advantage.

Most promotional schemes involve what is known as 'merchandising', where the strategy is to achieve a short term boost in sales. One of the most typical is what is known as the 'Self Liquidating Premium' offer. With an SLP something is offered free with your product in return for some proof of purchase – for example, saving the packet tops of a grocery item, to exchange for another product.

Although this may sound costly, it may be no more expensive than offering discounts, because with an SLP the idea is to get the consumer to pay the full price for your product, while you have obtained the special offer goods cheaply through wholesale or bulk buying.

SLPs may sound like the preserve of big business. But the principle of SLPs can be applied equally to small businesses. So, for that matter, can other merchandising deals such as free offers and discounts. To return to the example of the landscape gardener – you might like to make the special promotional offer of free window cleaning for anyone who books you in the next four weeks.

Offering a chance to sample your product(s) is another obvious promotional tool, but is only really applicable with low cost products such as food and drink. It can be expensive and needs to be restricted to specific promotional drives at, say, exhibitions or the point of sale.

Public relations

Few small businesses will think to bother about public relations when they start out. But for businesses with a local customer base, PR is another useful form of marketing.

For a start, you should consider sending press releases to the local newspapers and radio stations. These are simply short write-ups about your business and its products. These days the media loves stories about entrepreneurs. Getting space in newspapers and time on the radio in this way is free advertising.

You should also think about involvement in the local community. For fairly small amounts of money you might be able to sponsor local fêtes, sports days or exhibitions. In return you will get your company name prominently displayed for everyone to see.

Marketing and advertising budgets

It is amazing how many small business ventures start out without setting aside a budget for marketing. It should be stressed that unless you are extremely lucky, one of the hardest parts of business is building up market awareness. Without a planned marketing campaign of some sort most businesses will struggle to survive. Even if you start in business with what seems like a satisfactory amount of work, don't neglect the marketing side. Take your eye off the market for even a short while and you are likely to find that the order book will soon become empty. Ideally, your business plan should set aside a percentage of expected sales to cover what you are going to spend on marketing and advertising. This amount can then be adjusted as your experience of the market develops. Some product areas will need more to be spent on advertising than others. Making your business subservient to the marketplace – to think 'customer' all the time – is a very large part of business success.

8. Terms of trading

Obtaining that first sale is a major achievement for anyone who is self-employed or running a small business. Your business is working, but in terms of your business survival you have only just started. It is a sad fact of life that nothing is quite so abused in terms of trading as the small business.

The very fact that you are new on the business scene, vulnerable, dependent on others and probably without the strength to fight injustices means that many will aim to exploit you. However, as long as you are prepared, you will probably be okay.

Giving credit to customers

The first big shock to most self-starters in business is that it can take a very long time for anyone to pay you for the product or service which you have sold them. Unless you are in a cash business, like retailing where you receive payment at the point of sale, you can expect to wait anything up to three months, and sometimes even longer, for your customers to pay up. This is almost the norm for manufacturing businesses, with their big-business customers invariably the worst offenders.

Small manufacturers should expect their debtors (those who owe them money) to amount to around 40% of their annual sales in their first few years. The government is trying to find ways of imposing penalties on late payers, but don't expect much to change.

The important thing is to be alert to late payment, try to get around it somehow, and make sure that your cash flow projections have allowed for your customers' tardy payment procedures.

The norm is that a business, or individual, won't pay early unless there are some conditions laid down by the supplier. This is not to say that those conditions won't often be ignored. But stating your terms of payment when you invoice makes a good start.

Prompt invoicing

'Payment within 30 days' is a reasonable request to make when invoicing. But make sure you send an invoice with, or very soon after, delivery of the product, or completion of the service. It is amazing how many self-employed and freelance people don't even bother to invoice at all. Somehow they think payment will just be sent to them. Any established business will find it next to impossible to pay without an invoice. The invoice should give the date of the order, the customer's name, address and order number, the amount of money owing – including any VAT – the date of delivery and the expected date of payment. Many self-employed and new small businesses will leave the latter off through sheer timidity. Being pushy might lose precious business surely? Better, however, to be pushy and lose those customers whose late payment practices will threaten the very survival of your business.

Many businesses will expect to receive a statement at the end of a month, which repeats the terms on the invoice. Certainly, if payment has not been received by the end of a month, send a statement. This applies to one-person businesses as much as to small incorporated firms.

Failure to pay

What if your customer has failed to pay within the specified time? Getting angry too soon is fruitless. If payment has failed to materialise after one month send a polite letter, again setting out the terms of payment. If another month elapses without payment send another letter. After that you can threaten legal action and this will usually elicit payment. But don't bother taking legal action for amounts less than £100; solicitors' fees will make it uneconomic. All businesses carry bad debts to some degree.

Debt collection agencies can be used, but you had best discover their tactics before employing one.

Factoring

Small businesses can make use of what are known as factoring companies to protect them against the dangers to cash flow which are inherent in late payment. A factoring company will advance you money against your sales ledger in return for a fee. The factor then has the responsibility of chasing up your debts.

Factoring is a growing force in business and its biggest applications are to businesses with sales of over £50,000 and under £1 million. But it is not cheap. Usually a factor will agree to cover 80% of your book debts for a fee that can range between ½–5% of turnover. Factoring only suits a certain type of business.

Remember, although factors are not in the same class as debt collectors they are, to an extent, prying into the business of your precious customers.

Factoring best suits small firms with a large number of customers buying relatively low priced goods. For further information about factoring contact:

Association of British Factors,
147 Fleet Street,
London EC4A 2BU.
Tel: 01-583 0265

Credit control

Most small businesses that go bust do so not because they don't have good business ideas or because there isn't a market for their products. They usually simply run out of cash. Good cash flow forecasting (see chapter 4) can provide warnings about impending cash crises. But without a system that reacts to a company's credit situation, things will go wrong and will not be righted.

In most cases a small business's credit controller is going to be the proprietor. In other words, you. Here are some simple guidelines to make sure you are watching your creditors properly:

- Be prepared to deal with customers who exceed their credit limits. Establish reminder procedures.
- Set credit limits for customers, i.e. they cannot have more than a certain amount outstanding at any one time.
- Enquire about the creditworthiness of customers before granting them credit.
- Make sure your statements give details of how long the balances have been outstanding.
- Check whether the amounts owing from your debtors is increasing as a proportion of sales. If it is, you need to tighten your credit control.

Giving discounts

Most businesses offer discounts on the list price of products or services. This can be done as part of a promotion or as a special incentive to particular customers.

You should be willing to give discounts for purchases in bulk. It is also sometimes a good idea to offer discounts for anyone who pays 'cash on delivery'. But don't be hounded into giving uneconomical discounts. Unless your marketing strategy is to sell some lines as 'loss leaders', creating the precedent of giving a discount can be dangerous. Always make it clear that you are allowing the discount for a special reason. In other words, make sure that you are getting something in return.

This is where you should refer to your breakeven pricing calculation (see chapter 6). Discounts are usually given for volume sales, as economies-of-scale generally mean that the more you produce of something, the cheaper its unit cost of production. But do the calculation again, this time working with the discounted price, and see if you are still going to break even or, better still, fulfil your objective of making a profit.

Obtaining credit from suppliers

It would be nice to think that because your customers demand credit from you, that you, in turn, might expect credit from your suppliers. Unfortunately, this is not always the case.

Because you are unlikely to be a major buyer many suppliers, particularly large firms, will be reluctant to offer you special terms. Indeed, it is not unknown for some large firms to ask the proprietors of small businesses for personal guarantees to cover the credit which is being extended to them.

But there is no reason why you should not be entrepreneurial about your buying strategies. After all, the fact that you are likely to be granted less credit from your suppliers than your customers will demand from you, makes it seem logical that, ultimately, you are going to get squeezed in the middle.

Here are some guidelines which you should follow when dealing with suppliers:

- Always ask for the maximum credit terms you can get.
- Enquire about discounts for cash on delivery.
- Ask about discounts for bulk orders.
- Shop around amongst suppliers for the best terms.
- Ask about possible barter deals, i.e. can you sell the supplier your product or service in return, or part return, for supplies.
- Ask about hire purchase, rental or lease deals where appropriate.

The basic philosophy behind all of the foregoing is to keep cash in your business for as long as possible. It is a basic law of business survival and, remember, most businesses go under because they run out of cash.

9. Keeping the books

Only limited companies are legally required to keep proper books detailing all payments and receipts of cash, amounts owed and owing and the company's assets. But any business, even sole traderships, should get into the habit of keeping up-to-date books from the beginning. Many entrepreneurs, who by nature prefer to get on with the business of making sales, find book-keeping a chore. But a reluctance to keep financial records is very often the reason why businesses fail. Until you can monitor your business's financial condition it is impossible to make sensible decisions about pricing, credit control and financing. There are few bank managers who will be prepared to loan money to a business which cannot produce evidence of its book-keeping discipline. And the existence of accurate financial records will make dealing with the Inland Revenue and Customs & Excise that much simpler.

Getting organised

The first thing you should do when setting up a business is open a business bank account. This applies equally to a sole trader and an incorporated company. Any money which you, the proprietor, take out of the account will be classed as 'drawings' and should be itemised as such.

Secondly, be prepared to start recording expenses which you incur in the running of your business. It is very easy to forget to list expenses, particularly things like tickets for travelling which do not automatically come with a receipt. So get into the habit of taking a notebook around with you in which you can immediately enter details of all expenses. And get a file in which you can keep all invoices in date order.

The cash book

The cash book is the central item of most small business accounting systems. It records all receipts and payments which go through your business bank account. It is thus recording all transactions made by cheque. It will also record deposits of cash which you make into the bank account, if you are running a cash business such as a shop. Be careful to note any receipts or payments covered by standing orders.

There are many types of cash book available from stationers, although you can quite easily draw one up yourself using a plain notebook. Entries in a typical cash book will look like this:

Cash Book (Receipts) £						
Date	Payer	Total	VAT	Sales	Invoice No.	Other income
2.5.87	J.Jones	50.00	7.50	42.50	20	
4.5.87	T.Ltd	80.00	12.00	68.00	21	
9.5.87	B.Ltd	40.00	6.00	34.00	23	
15.5.87	A.Watt	70.00	10.50	59.50	25	
20.5.87	C.Ltd	18.00				18.00 (refund)
27.5.87	S.Ltd	100.00	15.00	85.00	22	
		358.00	51.00	289.00		18.00

Cash Book (Payments) £							
Date	Payee	V. No.	Total	VAT	Supplies	Rent	Drawings
5.5.87	Z.Ltd	166	115.00	15.00	100.00		
11.5.87	L.Ltd	241	57.50	7.50	50.00		
17.5.87	U.Ltd	–	230.00	30.00	200.00		
25.5.87	Prop.		200.00				200.00
27.5.87	Wages & NIC		100.00		100.00		
29.5.87	Rental	324	150.00			150.00	
			852.50	52.50	450.00	150.00	200.00

The type of entry columns in the cash book can vary according to your type of business. Note that it is always important to take out the VAT element in all receipts and payments. This makes your VAT returns easy to complete. Anything you draw out of the business account for your own personal purposes must be listed under 'drawings', as must your salary, listed in the example of payments opposite as 'Prop.' for Proprietor's expenses. The term 'supplies' can include any items required in the running of your business.

Wages come under the heading of 'supplies', although in the cash book you will only enter the net wages figure, i.e. after deduction of income tax and National Insurance contributions.

At the end of every month or week, you should total up the amounts and arrive at your latest cash balance. In the example above, the business's bank account would end the month of May 1987 with a net cash outflow of £852.50 − £358 = £494.50. This is the figure you should check against your cash flow forecast (see chapter 4) to see whether your cash position is as you have predicted.

Petty cash book

For accounting purposes cheques, as well as notes and coins, are referred to as 'cash'. But when a lot of your trade is in notes and coins you must keep a separate petty cash book which details 'cash in' on the left hand side, and 'cash out' on the right hand side. Keep the receipts for anything you buy with cash, along with petty cash vouchers that detail these withdrawals.

If all your business is in notes and coins then just totalling up the money in and out will give you a cash balance. If you also do business with cheques, then the 'cash position' of your business will be the sum of the cash book (see above) and the petty cash book. This means that when cash reflected in the petty cash book is deposited or withdrawn from your bank account, it will be entered in the cash book.

Sales purchase ledgers

It may appear that a cash book and a petty cash book enable a business to control every detail of its financial affairs.

But a cash book does not tell you either what you are owed by your debtors or what you owe to your suppliers and creditors. Invoices being received for payment need to be listed in date order and a note made of the date payment was made and the VAT (which will later be reclaimable if you are registered for VAT). Similarly, if you are running a business which issues invoices for work done and which grants credit to customers, you need to list invoices issued, in date order, the VAT charged and when payment was received.

This kind of information is required by law in an incorporated business but any business should keep similar records. The advantages of keeping a sales/purchase ledger are that:

- It permits you to calculate your sales for any period.
- It enables you quickly to add up your declarable and reclaimable VAT.
- It permits ready identification of late-payers and your own trade debts.

The type of sales and purchase ledger you keep will depend on the complexity of your business. Some sales ledgers will have separate pages for each customer or supplier. This allows you instantly to see what you have paid a particular supplier against what you owe. You can check this against the statements which you receive from that supplier. Similarly, on the sales side you can see what a customer has paid for and which invoices are still awaiting payment. This makes it easy to work out statements when you send them to your customers.

This is obviously a useful type of ledger if you are doing a lot of business with a select number of customers or suppliers. A simpler system might look like the example below.

Purchases (£)							
Date received	Invoice date	Supplier	Amount	VAT	Total	Date paid	Voucher number
8.5.87	6.5.87	Gas B.	156.00	–	156.00	1.6.87	343
18.5.87	15.5.87	B. Ltd	80.00	12.00	92.00	1.6.87	101
22.5.87	21.5.87	G. Ltd	230.00	34.50	264.50	3.7.87	978
24.5.87	21.5.87	Elec.	123.00	–	123.00	5.7.87	956
26.5.87	22.5.87	X. Ltd	47.00	7.05	54.05	6.7.87	378

Sales (£)						
Date delivered	Customer	Invoice number	Amount	VAT	Total	Date received
12.5.87	P. Ltd	23	60.00	9.00	69.00	1.7.87
17.5.87	L. Ltd	24	40.00	6.00	46.00	26.6.87
21.5.87	Z. Ltd	25	120.00	18.00	138.00	18.9.87
27.5.87	A. Ltd	26	85.00	12.75	95.75	2.7.87
29.5.87	Q. Ltd	27	20.00	3.00	23.00	3.7.87

You can add other columns to give more detail if you wish. You can, for example, list what type of goods were supplied or delivered and it is sometimes a good idea to make a note of cheque numbers.

The most obvious virtue of this kind of day-by-day record of sales and purchases is that you can very quickly add up your VAT figures for the quarterly returns (see chapter 10). Customs & Excise will need to know both the VAT declarable (on your sales) and the VAT reclaimable (on your purchases).

Payroll records

If your business is taking on employees, the Inland Revenue will require annual submissions of the relevant information. The figures you should keep are:
- Basic pay.
- Any other pay, overtime, bonuses etc.
- Total or gross pay which is taxable.
- PAYE deductions.
- Employees' National Insurance.
- Total deductions.
- Net pay paid.
- Employer's National Insurance.

Most stationers stock record-keeping books for payroll purposes.

Other book-keeping procedures

You should discuss with your accountant exactly what level of book-keeping is relevant to your business. For most businesses the

systems outlined in this chapter will be sufficient. A limited company will, however, also be required to maintain a capital or asset register which
records the purchase and disposal of such things as property, plant and machinery.

When an accountant looks at the various books described here he will compile a 'nominal ledger' where purchases and sales are balanced to provide a 'trial balance'. The trial balance also provides a complete list of all transactions during a given period. Once a trial balance has been arrived at, your accountant can produce a 'profit and loss' statement and a 'balance sheet' (see chapter 11).

Who should do the books?

In most small businesses the proprietor invariably does the book-keeping at the start. As long as a proper system is set up at the beginning this is not the onerous task it often sounds. Later you may get your spouse or someone else you trust to help, until eventually you may employ a clerk qualified in book-keeping. If you become an incorporated business you will get your auditor – who is usually with the same firm as your account – to work with your book-keeper and maintain a regular control over the figures.

If your business is going to need the use of a computer from the outset it is worth investigating some of the book-keeping and accounting software packages which are on the market. Ask your accountant's advice, to make sure you are using mutually compatible systems.

10. Dealing with the VAT man

Value Added Tax is often seen as one of business's heaviest burdens. To self-employed people and small businesses VAT can certainly be time-consuming and frustrating to deal with. But as chapter 9 shows, most of the problems which arise with VAT can be simply avoided by up-to-date and thorough book-keeping. Indeed, VAT should be a fairly straightforward affair for the majority of the self-employed and small firms. First-timers in business should not be frightened off by the spectre of VAT returns and the dreaded VAT inspection. Customs & Excise, which administers VAT, can be fairly flexible about the individual requirements of certain businesses and you should contact your local VAT office if in any doubt about the tax.

What is VAT?

VAT is a sales tax chargeable on taxable 'supplies' and is ultimately payable by the consumer. It is the responsibility of the provider of the goods or services to levy the VAT and return it to H.M. Customs & Excise in a given accounting period. The standard rate of VAT is currently 15%. There are two types of VAT to be considered:

- Output tax. This is the 15% VAT which the business charges on its goods or services and which it must return to Customs & Excise.
- Input tax. This is the VAT which the business pays on its own purchases of goods and services and which can, in most circumstances (see below), be recovered by offsetting it against output tax.

Am I liable for VAT?

If you believe your sales are going to exceed £21,300 per annum, or have exceeded £7,250 in any calendar quarter, you must register for VAT with Customs & Excise. You are required to notify Customs & Excise within 30 days of becoming liable for VAT. The tax applies equally to self-employed sole traders, partnerships and incorporated businesses.

Customs & Excise talk about 'taxable persons' for VAT purposes. This means that all businesses carried out by the same person must

65

be taken into account when calculating liability for VAT. Sometimes a business which is paying high levels of VAT input tax can register for VAT voluntarily even if it has not reached the £21,300 sales level.

Traders who delay approaching Customs & Excise may have to pay penalties and this means that they will be assessed for VAT without being able to recover it from customers.

Zero rating and exemption

Some goods and services are 'zero-rated' for VAT, which means that you don't have to charge any VAT on sales. But a business in a zero-rated sector can still claim back its VAT input tax. Obviously businesses making zero-rated supplies are in the best possible position with VAT, since they are in a position to receive VAT rebates.

The main zero-rated groups are: most food items but not pet foods and alcoholic drinks, water supplies except distilled and bottled water, books, talking books for the blind, news services, fuel and power, and the sale of buildings.

Other goods and services are described as 'exempt' from VAT and, where no VAT is chargeable, a business making exempt supplies is not permitted to reclaim its VAT input tax.

The main exempt groups are: land sales unless falling into the zero-rated sector, insurance, postal services, betting, financial services, education, health, burial and cremation, and trade union and professional bodies.

These definitions of zero-rated and exempt supplies are general. Traders should make detailed enquiries through H.M. Customs & Excise to discover which category their supplies fall into. A business can find that it is supplying a mixture of taxable, zero-rated and exempt supplies. This makes calculating input tax recovery very complex, and is one of the problems which has given VAT a bad name.

Partial exemption

If a business is making supplies of both VATable and exempt goods or services it is described as 'partially exempt'. Clearly, a business making some exempt supplies will not be able to recover as much input tax as it could if it supplied totally VATable or zero-rated items. Customs & Excise is continually reviewing the methods used to calculate the deduction of input tax on partially exempt businesses. For small businesses there is usually little to worry about.

At present if that part of input tax which is attributable to exempt supplies is less than:

£100 a month on average; or

both £250 a month on average and 50% of all input tax; or

both £500 a month on average and 25% of all input tax, then you can treat that tax as though it was attributable to taxable supplies.

VAT for retailers

Retailers often find themselves selling a mixture of zero-rated, exempt and VATable goods. Because they are often taking cash for sales it is impossible for retailers to keep details of all their transactions. Today, some modern types of cash tills can help shopkeepers with their VAT. But Customs & Excise have had to devise nine special schemes – lettered 'A' to 'J' (I is omitted) – for retailers, which are based on systems for calculating gross takings.

It's sensible to discuss which scheme might be most suitable for you with Customs & Excise, although you aren't obliged to use any of the schemes if you have an alternative method. The official schemes *are* probably the best systems, however, because they guard against you paying too much VAT. Once you have chosen to use a retail VAT scheme you are obliged to stick to it for one year. This is binding in law.

Imports and exports

VAT is imposed on imports on the basis of their market value. Payment is either by cash at the port of entry or under special duty deferment systems for VAT-registered traders. The latter involve payments being delayed until the 15th day of the month following importation. The importer pays by direct debit from its bank account. With imported services, VAT is only applied to certain types, and only the partly exempt business will usually incur a VAT cost.

Goods exported from the UK are zero-rated but input VAT can still be recovered. This makes exporting attractive because of the better VAT input relief. You must provide proof of export, through shipping documents, within three months of the supply taking place.

Registering for VAT

When you inform Customs & Excise of your liability for VAT you will be sent form VAT1. This needs to be completed with details of your business, when it started, your expectations of sales, and your bank sorting code and account number or National Giro number. The form must be submitted to the VAT office local to your business.

In return you will be sent a certificate of registration, VAT 4, which will give you your registration number and details of when, and how frequently, you must start submitting your VAT returns.

The tax point

It is important to understand what Customs & Excise mean by the 'tax point' for VAT purposes. The tax point is the moment in time when a sale becomes liable for VAT. The tax point does not depend on when goods or services were ordered, or the date of payment.

A tax point is created whenever you issue an invoice. That means you will have to pay Customs & Excise the VAT due at the end of that quarter regardless of whether you receive payment against the invoice. It may pay you to delay invoicing and thus move the tax point in a way which will preserve cash flow.

Customs & Excise permit the invoice date to become the tax point if an invoice is issued within 14 days from the date of removal or delivery of the goods. This also applies to services, although there will be separate tax points on invoicing for various types of continuous service.

If a payment has been received prior to removal of the goods or performance of the service, the earlier date becomes the tax point, but only on the amount received. Goods sold on sale-or-return don't attract a tax point until the goods have been adopted by the customer.

Cash accounting

By the autumn of 1987 it is hoped that small businesses with sales of below £250,000 per annum will have the option of accounting for their VAT on the basis of cash paid and received. This could have obvious cash flow advantages for small companies who struggle to obtain payment from customers. It would also give automatic relief against bad debts.

Keeping VAT records

Keeping a complete record of all your business transactions, showing input and output VAT, is essential. If you don't keep records Customs & Excise can make a VAT assessment on the strength of what they think you should pay. Without records, it will be very difficult to convince them that they have made an error.

Recording VAT inputs and outputs in the cash book and the sales and purchase ledger was shown in chapter 9. It can be advisable to maintain a separate VAT account if the number of transactions during a year is particularly high. Keep all invoices on which you have paid VAT input tax and copies of your sales invoices on which you have charged your output VAT. Customs & Excise can now require records to be kept for up to six years. For each VAT accounting period, which is usually quarterly, work out the difference between your output tax and your input tax to complete your VAT return.

Invoicing your sales

Except for retailers, if you are taxable for VAT you must issue VAT invoices in a standard format for all supplies which are made to other taxable persons. The invoices must carry your VAT number, as your customers will need it to reclaim the VAT they have paid you. Additionally, the invoice must state:

- Invoice number.
- The tax point.
- Customer's name and address.
- Whether it is a sale or hire purchase, loan, lease or rental, etc.
- The quantity of goods of each description and rate of VAT.
- Total amount payable, excluding VAT.
- Total amount of VAT chargeable.
- Total amount payable, including VAT.

Making VAT returns

VAT returns are usually made every three months, with the timing dependent on your own financial year. Returns should be submitted within one month of the end of the accounting period. If you are persistently late with your returns heavy surcharges are likely to be imposed. In 1988, however, there is a plan to permit small businesses with sales of less than £250,000 per annum, which have been VAT registered for at least one year, to make a single VAT return. The idea is that you would make nine equal payments on account through direct debit, plus a tenth balancing payment when you make an annual return. The tenth payment would be made two months after the end of the accounting year when you submit the return. The instalments would be calculated on the basis of the net VAT you paid in the preceding year with adjustments for expected changes in your business in the current year.

It pays to make prompt submission of your VAT return. If your input credits exceed your output VAT you can receive a refund of the excess within 14 days of submitting your return. This would obviously enhance your business's cash position. Some zero-rated businesses can ask to submit their returns on a monthly basis if the cash flow advantages of receiving their input credits are too attractive to be missed.

VAT inspections

Customs & Excise will make on the spot investigations of a company's VAT records when it sees fit. They will usually inform you beforehand of their intention to visit and it is advisable to notify your accountant who could, if you prefer, handle the entire proceedings. Most businesses will be visited during their first year of registration and can expect return calls from the inspectors every three years or so. The inspectors are checking that you maintain adequate VAT records. If your book-keeping systems are in order you should have little to fear.

Enquiries about your own particular VAT requirements, and for booklets on VAT, should be addressed to:

The VAT Central Unit,
Alexander House,
21 Victoria Avenue,
Southend-on-Sea, SS99 1AA.
Tel: 0702 348944

11. Using an accountant

Finding a good accountant and using his or her services to the full is one of the wisest moves you can make. The accountancy profession has changed a great deal in recent years and is under growing competitive pressure to offer a full range of services to the self-employed and small business community. The problem over the years is that traders have had a limited perception of what accountants can do for them. The self-employed have seen them as little more than people who advise about claiming tax relief for expenses or how to fill in their tax return. Small incorporated firms usually feel that their accountants never bother to really understand their businesses and are simply the people who perform the once-a-year statutory audit.

Admittedly, there are differing degrees of ability amongst accountants and they all tend to have their own specialities which may, or may not, make them suitable to your particular business. There is also the question of whether to go for the small local accountant, the medium-sized regional accountant or the big national groups who boast expertise in practically every area you can imagine.

Remember, you're paying the accountant's fees and it's up to you who you use, and what you ask them to do. Just as with banks, you're under no obligation to stick with the same practitioner if you're not satisfied with the service.

What an accountant can do

Depending on your type of business – sole trader, partnership, limited company – accountants should be able to help with a wide range of subjects. For the average first-timer in business, your accountant will probably be your most important adviser. Your accountant will be able to help on:

- Business structure and incorporation.
- Raising finance and construction of a business plan.
- Establishing book-keeping and financial reporting systems.
- Cash flows and forecasting, provision of management accounts.
- Purchase of property and other assets, leases, hire purchase and rentals.
- Personal, corporate and VAT tax planning.

- Share structure, share options, dividends and directors' remuneration.
- Audit provision with profit-and-loss accounts, balance sheets etc.
- Insurance and pensions.
- Purchase of computer systems.
- General management consultancy.

Don't expect every accountant to be proficient in each of these areas. With the possible exception of the big national and international firms, they won't. But when choosing an accountant ask yourself about your requirements over the next few years. If you are going to remain a sole trader for the foreseeable future then a local accountant who specialises in the self-employed will probably suffice. But if you intend to grow rapidly, become an incorporated business, take on more staff and go for the big time then it might as well select a larger firm of accountants from the outset.

What do accountants charge?

Accountants' fees vary enormously and very few bother to describe the basis on which they charge. But you should ask about the fee structure before you decide whether you wish to become a client. Very broadly, a self-employed person may need to pay little more than £200 a year for an accountant's services. Advice about claiming tax relief on business expenses and on making income tax returns under Schedule D will not normally require a great deal of an accountant's time.

Where accountants' fees start to mount up is when a business becomes incorporated or needs a wider range of advice, or when a statutory audit has to be performed. Accountants usually charge by the hour. This could be anywhere between £20 to £100, sometimes more. An audit can cost between £2,000 and £10,000, but for the average small firm the lower end of the scale is more usual. It all depends on how much you wish to draw upon your accountant's time and your business's own financial resources.

Questions sole traders and partners should ask their accountant

Should I (we) be thinking about incorporating the business? Your accountant will need to assess the personal tax positions of the proprietor or partners. If your marginal rate of income tax exceeds the marginal rate of corporation tax, then it might pay to incorporate. But sole traders and partners have more opportunity to claw back trading losses against previous income.

Where should I (we) go to raise finance? The chances are that your accountant will advise you to try straight bank finance. But should it be overdraft or loan? If you set up an incorporated business perhaps your accountant knows of private investors who want to subscribe for equity in small local companies?

What sort of book-keeping systems should I (we) set up? Since your accountant has to scrutinise your figures, make sure that he has suggested the system you are going to use in the first place. Get your accountant to talk you through the simple cash book and sales and purchase ledger procedures.

How will I (we) be assessed for Income Tax? Traders are assessed for Income Tax on a prior year basis, i.e. on profits arising in a period which ends in the previous fiscal year. Because this is impossible when a business starts there can be advantages in timing the beginning of your accounting date so that you get maximum deferment of taxation. Also ask about claiming tax rebates on your previous years' income, if your business makes losses in any of its first four years.

When should I (we) register for VAT? Even though a trader need not register for VAT until his annual turnover exceeds £21,300 per annum, there can be advantages of voluntary registration before this level is exceeded in order to recoup input VAT. See chapter 10.

What expenses can I (we) claim against tax? There is a long list of expenses which are tax deductible. They include:

- Accountants' fees.
- Advertising.
- Bad debts.
- Bank charges.
- Rent, rates, heating and lighting.
- Repairs, insurance, cleaning, postage, stationery, telephone.
- Hire charges.
- Pension contributions.
- Employees' wages.
- Travel expenses.
- Uniforms and special clothing.

Ask your accountant how to record all these expenses.

What happens if family members join the business? Theoretically, there are savings to be made by introducing others to share in the profits of a company, because of the benefits arising from lower bands of tax. But there can be problems if the business has to cease and then start again for tax purposes.

What about pensions? Apart from the state pension the self-employed have to make their own provisions for retirement. If a pension is of high importance to you it might be better to form an incorporated business where pensions are easier to build up. Otherwise seek advice about private pension schemes where you can contribute up to 17½% of your annual earnings.

Questions incorporated businesses should ask their accountants

How much should the directors pay themselves? This can be a difficult area for many small companies, but directors' salaries can be deductible against Corporation Tax if they are seen to be in proportion to the contribution the directors make to the business. Would it be more advantageous to be paid in dividends? With basic rate Income Tax now at the same level as the small company Corporation Tax level of 27%, it may make little sense to pay directors' salaries of over £17,900 as these will attract more tax than money retained in the business.

What are the tax implications of the company making a loss? Exactly what profits a private company chooses to declare are usually a matter for internal debate. Tax losses can be carried forward, however, and can be very handy in offsetting any Capital Gains Tax.

When will the company have to pay Corporation Tax? The Inland Revenue is now asking companies to speed up their payments of Corporation Tax. Companies will now be required to pay Corporation Tax nine months after the end of their accounting period, regardless of whether an assessment has been made. Your accountant will need to be fast off the mark with advice on tax planning.

When is the company liable for Capital Gains Tax? A company pays Corporation Tax on capital gains as well as on its profits. Recent changes in the way Capital Gains Tax is levied makes tax planning even more essential for some small companies, because there could be an increased danger of stepping above the small company tax rate.

What happens when the company wants to start paying dividends?
Most small incorporated businesses won't necessarily want to pay
dividends for some while, but there could be tax advantages in
paying directors' remuneration in dividends rather than salary.
You will need an accountant's advice on the payment of Advance
Corporation Tax on dividends which, if the company is not already
paying Corporation Tax, will become an additional cost.

What are the best remuneration packages for employees? Your
accountant should help you in setting up your payroll and PAYE
systems. But you may want to make incentives to your employees
in the form of cars, medical insurance, pensions or through
participation in share option schemes. You will need to find out
what are taxable benefits, which are tax free and where it is more
advantageous to the company in tax terms to provide 'perks' of this
kind rather than cash benefits.

How do we set up a group pension scheme? You will need to find out
which pension schemes qualify for Inland Revenue 'exempt' status
and which, therefore, allow employers' contributions to be
deductible against profits. In some self-administered pension
schemes it is possible to lend part of the funds back to the business
as a form of financing the company.

Understanding profit and loss accounts

One of the principal functions of an accountant is to draw up an
annual profit and loss account and, in the case of incorporated
businesses, a balance sheet. The accountant produces the profit
and loss account and balance sheet from the books which you have
maintained throughout the year.

It is upon the evidence of a profit and loss document formulated
by your accountant that you are assessed for tax. Companies are
also assessed for tax in the same way.

Profit and loss accounts may sometimes look different in their
detail but they all basically say the same thing. The profit and loss is
simply an addition of all the money that has come into a business
during a period, minus the expenditure. A profit and loss account
can be prepared for quarters, half years or, more usually, for annual
periods.

A simplified profit and loss account might look like the example
on page 74.

XYZ Ltd Profit and Loss Account for period to year ending 31.12.87 (£)		
	1987	1986
Sales	65,000	53,000
Cost of sales	38,000	29,000
	27,000	24,000
Overheads	20,000	19,000
Net profit before tax	7,000	5,000

It is important to realise that 'sales' in a profit and loss account have nothing to do with whether all the money against invoices has actually been received. This is why cash flow budgets (see chapter 4) are so crucial in describing the true state of a company's liquidity. Here, 'sales' means when goods or services have actually been provided.

The 'cost of sales' relates to those items such as raw materials and labour costs which vary according to the level of sales being made.

By deducting cost of sales from sales you obtain a gross profit figure which, in the above example for XYZ Ltd in 1987, was £27,000.

'Overheads' are fixed costs like rent and rates and, after this figure is deducted from gross profit, you arrive at a net profit figure.

Understanding balance sheets

Accountants must draw up an annual balance sheet for incorporated businesses. Although there are simplified requirements for small companies with sales of below £1.4m per annum, a balance sheet total of less than £700,000 or employing less than 50 people (or a combination of two of these factors) the basic arithmetic is the same as for big corporations. A simplified balance sheet might look like the example on the opposite page.

XYZ Ltd Balance Sheet at 31.12.87 (£)		
Fixed assets		30,000
Current assets		
Stock	39,000	
Debtors	37,000	
Cash at bank	700	
	76,700	
Current liabilities	11,000	
Net current assets		65,700
Net assets		95,700
Financed by:		
Share capital		35,000
Retained profits or losses		5,000
Loan capital		55,700
		95,700

A balance sheet shows what a company is doing with its money and where it has got that money from. It only reflects the financial situation for that one day when the figures were compiled.

In the above example you can see that the money that has gone into the business is the £95,700 at the bottom of the right hand column. This is made up from: 'share capital', which is the money put into the business by its founder directors or other equity investors; 'retained profits', which is what the company made after paying its taxes in the previous year; and 'loan capital' which is what the company has borrowed on set loans (as opposed to overdraft).

Above this you can see how that money is accounted for, or balanced, by the activities of the company. 'Fixed assets' (plant, machinery, freeholds), accounts for £30,000 of the company's worth. A company's 'current assets' are made up of things which are continually changing, such as its 'stocks', its 'debtors' (those who owe the company money) and its balance of 'cash' at the bank. In the case of XYZ Ltd, you can see that its current assets total £76,700.

'Current liabilities' is that money which the company owes, principally to trade creditors, and which has to be deducted from current assets to arrive at a figure for 'net current assets'. The net current asset figure is in the right hand column for additions and totals £65,700.

By adding net current assets to fixed assets you end up with a 'net asset' figure (£95,700) which is the value of the business and which has to equal the 'financed by' figure at the bottom of the balance sheet.

The audit

Most small companies seem to dread 'audit time'. This is the day of judgement as far as the book-keeper is concerned. But you should make sure that your accountant, who will usually (but not always) be your auditor, has advised you how to prepare your books for audit. There is no use spending the year compiling figures in one way, only to find that your auditor wants them prepared differently. Also establish before you take on an accountant how long after the end of your financial year he can perform the audit. Many businesses wait far longer than necessary.

12. Using a solicitor

Few people going into business for the first time think of getting a solicitor on their side. Indeed, unless you have used a solicitor to help in the formation of an incorporated company or the construction of a partnership agreement, the chances are that you won't go out and find one until your first case in the county court comes up – when you will most likely be trying to recover a bad debt.

Rather than waiting until a legal issue strikes, it is worth making enquiries about legal advice from the outset. Many high street solicitors will have little experience with the law affecting business and companies and you may have to look outside your local area to find someone with the right competence. And, as with accountants, fees can vary a lot. You may pay £50 an hour for legal advice from a local solicitor but if you are dealing with a top London firm, its senior partners could charge £140 an hour or more.

Knowing of a good solicitor in case you need him is a sensible security, but there is no substitute for becoming familiar with the basic laws which affect business yourself. Here is a summary of the legal issues most likely to confront you at some point. (Employment law is discussed in chapter 16).

The business contract

Selling a product or service means that you are entering into a legal 'contract' with that customer. Nothing needs to be written down to make this contract legally binding. A sales order placed over the telephone is still a contract. All that needs to happen for a contract of sale to exist is:

- Someone to 'offer' something for sale.
- Someone to 'accept' that offer and agree payment.

Most of the legal obligations placed upon you as the seller are contained in The Sale of Goods Act 1979. This Act says you must:

- Sell goods of 'merchantable quality' and 'fit for any particular purpose' which the buyer has been told about. This means they must do what the buyer expects them to do.
- The goods must also be 'as described'. A box containing 90 nails, but described as containing 100, is a breach of the Act.

Customers are entitled to return goods and demand a refund where the article is defective, unfit for its purpose or when the seller has said to the customer he can return it if unsatisfactory. A business cannot get around the customer's right to return goods by putting up signs saying 'no refunds'.

If a customer cancels a contract you can, in theory, make a claim for the profit which you have lost. But this only applies if the item was in plentiful supply. If the item was scarce, it is judged unreasonable for the business to obtain a profit from the customer because the item should be easily sold elsewhere.

Customers can cancel a contract without redress from the business if something has not been delivered on time. Additionally, customers could claim compensation for failure to deliver by a certain date, if a loss of profit can be proved. For example, if you were supplying a company with a machine repair service and failed to complete the job in the time promised, the company could ask for compensation if it has lost orders as a result.

Your own small print

You can guard against much possible litigation from customers by drawing up a list of 'terms and conditions of sale' which you should have written onto order forms or, when appropriate, displayed at the business address. But this is not a way of escaping your obligations under the law. The Unfair Contract Terms Act 1977 is very strict on exclusion clauses which appear to be an attempt to escape liability. Your solicitor should help you in drawing up terms and conditions. Some of the most important terms and conditions which the average business might use are:

- The right to revise prices without notice.
- The right to revise product descriptions and specifications.
- No liability for loss or damage.
- No liability for late delivery due to reasons outside the business's control.
- Date for settlement of invoice (i.e. within a month).

Prices, credit and hire purchase

You can, if you wish, run a business which only accepts payment in cash. This is probably impractical for most firms other than retailers, but there is no law that says you have to accept cheques or other non-cash means of payment. Nor does a company have to accept payment through the post – if a customer's cheque is lost in the post they must pay again.

If you have to supply quotations or estimates you should endeavour to stick to that price. The law is unclear on whether a quote or an estimate is legally binding. If you are unsure about the costing of a particular job, give an estimate rather than quote, because there is more scope to adjust your pricing later.

If your customer is VAT registered you must supply an invoice showing any VAT (see chapter 10) although this will only apply if your business is registered for VAT.

Retail businesses offering credit to customers require a licence under the Consumer Credit Act 1974 – check with a solicitor which type you need. Licences are also required for certain types of hire purchase, but not when your business is done with limited companies.

It is quite easy to be in breach of the Consumer Credit Act if you start offering special payment favours to customers, particularly if you prefer to receive payment in cash. It is worth talking to your bank manager about setting up procedures to handle payments by credit cards, rather than let deference to your customers' cash situation land you on the wrong side of the law.

The Trade Descriptions Act

It is very important to appreciate the wide scope of the Trade Descriptions Act. As most people are aware, the Act makes it an offence to make inaccurate statements about goods, services or prices. But a customer does not have to take you to court for prosecution to ensue. All someone has to do is inform the Trading Standards Office and a summons can be taken out against you in a local magistrates court. The penalties can be a fine, compensation to the customer and, sometimes, imprisonment.

Special care should be taken over claims about pricing. Price reductions must be real and you should be able to demonstrate that you have had items on sale at the normal price for a clearly defined period before you make the mark-down.

Customers who don't pay

Practically every business experiences at some time a customer who fails to pay. In the case of personal bankruptcies and corporate insolvencies there is probably little that you can do about recovering the money. Otherwise, after sending the customer at least three warning letters, you should instruct your solicitors to take action. You can take action yourself by going through the County Court if the amounts concerned are small. Bearing in mind solicitors' fees, ensure the claim is going to be worth your while pursuing.

Patents, copyright and trademarks

Protecting the original inventions, design, or product names on which your business is based can be a complex and time-consuming business. Patent law, in particular, becomes more complicated all the time and now EEC rulings provide an added dimension.

If you are going to seek the protection of a patent you should consider using patent agents who, in Britain, are highly qualified if expensive. Lodging a patent application through a patent agent could cost around £300. Clearly, you must check at the Patent Office that no such invention has been made before and if you have inadvertently disclosed your idea, say by chatting to friends, your right to a patent may be lost. Otherwise you can apply for a patent yourself from:

The Patent Office,
State House,
66-71 High Holborn,
London WC1R 4TP.
Tel: 01-831 2525

The basic procedure is that your patent application will be open for public scrutiny for 18 months after the application is made. Anyone then is in a position to claim that the idea is not new or simply unworthy of patent protection.

If you receive a patent you get sole rights to exploit your invention in Britain for a period of 20 years. After that anyone can make use of your invention since its working details are free for public inspection at the Patent Office.

Copyrights provide the weakest form of protection under the law. Anything original put on paper such as writing, drawings and designs can be protected by copyright. However, many would argue that the law is not very strict in this area. Parts of works can be copied sometimes without infringing copyright although the holder of the copyright has to grant permission in all cases.

82

The copyright line printed on the work should always conform to the convention:

© John Smith 1987

A trade mark is a symbol or name which lends identification to a particular product or range of products. You can prevent other businesses using your trade mark by registering it at the Trade Marks Registry of the Patents Office. For around £100 a trade mark agent will do it for you, and conduct a search at the Registry.

There is no obligation to register a trade mark and, indeed, some large firms who have never bothered to register their famous trade marks can still claim protection under the law against copying.

The Competition Act

Britain's laws encouraging fair competition are poor in comparison with those of other countries and have, in the past, offered little protection to small firms who frequently find themselves the victims of larger companies' undercutting practices. But the competition laws are being reviewed in Britain under pressure from the EEC, which has already started to legislate very strongly in favour of small businesses. For example, unfair price discrimination and exclusive dealing arrangements amongst suppliers and their big firm customers are becoming the subject of mounting concern. In serious cases it is worth asking your Euro MP or other EEC officials whether you can seek redress in the EEC courts.

Health and safety regulations

The government has become conscious of the need to simplify the various health and safety regulations in the case of small firms. Broadly there are more relaxed conditions applying to firms employing less than 20 people. The most important legislation in this area is the Health & Safety at Work Act 1974 which is designed to protect the working conditions of employees in any business regardless of its size.

The Factories Act and the Shops Act deal with certain types of business and make requirements in areas such as notification of accidents, display of notices and safety signs, fire precautions and inspectors' visits. Full information can be obtained from:

The Health & Safety Executive,
25 Chapel Street,
London NW1 5DT.
Tel: 01-262 3277

Businesses which need licences

Many types of business require a licence before they can start
trading. Granting of the licence can sometimes take a long time, so
you should check whether one is needed at an early stage in your
planning. In the majority of cases the licencing body is the local
authority, although it can alternatively be the police, central
government, gaming authorities or Office of Fair Trading. Most
licences are renewable annually, although the fees involved are
usually small. There is not enough room here to list all the
businesses which require licences but these are a few examples:

- Accommodation agencies.
- Alcohol production and sales.
- Most businesses involving animals, including pet shops.
- Betting shops and bingo halls.
- Cinemas.
- Providers of credit facilities.
- Debt collection agencies.
- Most food businesses.
- Hire businesses.
- Scrap metal dealers.
- Street traders.
- Taxi services.
- Theatres.

To check whether your business needs a licence, dial 100 and ask
for *Freefone Enterprise*.

Last word on the law

Although government is trying to ease legal burdens on small
businesses the new Insolvency Act introduced in 1986 has, in some
ways, made life even more hazardous. Most significantly, the
protection of 'limited liability' is now looking less robust. In the
past when companies became insolvent the directors of a business
were more or less free to walk away, leaving creditors unpaid and

their own exposure to the financial failure limited to any personal bank guarantees. Now, however, the law is alert to a new category of crime which it calls 'wrongful trading'. It is difficult to define 'wrongful trading', but in cases of insolvency where it can be shown that the directors of a company acted in a questionable manner, they can be made liable for debts and, in some cases, barred from becoming directors again for a period.

13. Dealing with the tax man

Taxation of the self-employed

If you become self-employed, the first thing to do is ensure that the Inland Revenue (IR) is satisfied that your business is genuinely conducted on a self-employed basis and, as such, qualifies for Schedule D income tax. Because there are such generous tax concessions for the self-employed, the Inland Revenue tries to keep as many people in the PAYE bracket as possible. You should be wary if the nature of your self-employment is such that you really only have one customer. The IR might decide that you are in reality an employee of that firm and should be treated as such for tax purposes.

Once you decide to become self-employed, write to the Inspector of Taxes at your old employer's tax office, inform him of your decision and send both copies of your P45. He will then inform *your* local tax office, which will send you a questionnaire to complete. This will require details of the name under which your business will trade, its starting date, whether you will have any employees and so on.

If you leave your job with a reasonable amount of time before the end of the tax year, you should be able to obtain a tax rebate at the end of the tax year. If, for example, your tax coding under PAYE is 240, you are entitled to earn £2,400 per year free of taxation, i.e. £200 per month. If you work for only the first six months of that year, you will have been allowed £1,200 of your taxable allowance. If you earn no further money under PAYE in that tax year, your earnings will be assessed at the end of the year and the full £2,400 will be allowed. However, tax is never this simple, since pensions and insurance contributions complicate matters, which brings us neatly back to chapter 11 – the need for a good accountant!

The choice of a start-date and thus your business's own accounting date can be important in terms of when you pay tax. You should consult your accountant to determine the best time to commence trading. Broadly, it pays to start a business early in the tax year because you are deferring taxation of that year's profits for the longest possible time. The self-employed pay tax on a prior-year basis, i.e. taxation for 1987/88 profits will be charged in January and July 1988. Schedule D tax assessments are payable in two half-yearly instalments, on 1 January and the following 1 July, based on profits of the accounting period which ended in the previous year of assessment.

As mentioned in chapter 2 the self-employed are not charged tax on what they actually draw out of the business for their own living expenses. If you are self-employed there are no such things as wages and salaries. You are assessed for tax on the profits of your business which remain after all costs and expenses have been deducted.

Thus, if you have made sales of £18,000 in your accounting year and total expenditure was £14,000 you would be assessed for tax on a profit of £4,000. This is regardless of how much you have drawn out of the business account as your own drawings.

Clearly, the key for anyone in self-employment is to keep their assessable profits as low as possible to leave the maximum amount available for personal drawings. This is where the need to maintain adequate records recording all business expenses is important in making sure that the business does not pay too much tax.

The list of items you can charge as legitimate business expenses is long (see chapter 11) but don't expect the Inland Revenue to leave everything you claim unchallenged. If you claim the cost of purchasing and using a car as a business expense, the IR will want to know what amount of its use is for private purposes and it will make an adjustment accordingly. Similarly, with domestic bills like heating, lighting, rent and rates, the Inland Revenue will only permit a deduction against profits in proportion to the amount of space in your home which is being used for business purposes.

When losses are made in the first four years of self-employment these losses can be offset against your income of the three years prior to the year in which the loss was made. If these losses are claimed within two years of the year in which the loss was incurred this can lead to substantial rebates of your previous Income Tax payments – an obvious assistance to the cash situation in the early years of a business.

The tax rates which are applied to a self-employed person are the same as those for anyone in employment. You pay the basic rate of 27% for income tax on income (or in your case, profits) up to £17,900 after which the higher rate bands apply. Personal allowances are also the same for self-employed people, and you should make sure that you claim everything to which you are entitled because allowances cannot be carried forward.

Taxation for partnerships

Partnerships are, broadly speaking, taxed in the same way as the self-employed, i.e. under Schedule D on profits and not on personal drawings.

Legally, each partner is liable for the total assessment for tax, but the Inland Revenue will separate out each partner's liability according to the profit-sharing arrangement of the partnership, and the individual partner's personal allowances and tax bands. The partnership can charge the full range of expenses open to a self-employed person and losses can similarly be claimed against prior year earnings. In the case of losses the partners, who must share the losses in the same proportion as they have agreed to share the profits, can elect separately how they wish to set off their own losses.

Corporation Tax for small companies

Incorporated businesses with taxable profit below £100,000 are, at the time of writing, required to pay Corporation Tax at a rate of 27%. Profits above £500,000 attract the full rate of corporation tax of 35%, and in the marginal relief area between £100,000 and £500,000 the benefit of the 27% is gradually reduced.

Just as with a business conducted on a self-employed basis, profits assessable for Corporation Tax are arrived at after deducting all chargeable expenses. One difference is that directors' salaries can also be charged as a trading expense. However, there is not the same freedom to exploit the use of early trading losses.

In an incorporated business you will not be able to relieve losses against your previous personal income. Instead losses can only be carried forward against trading profits arising from the same trade.

Corporation Tax is assessed on the income in each accounting period. The way in which companies pay their Corporation Tax is in the process of being tightened up and, in future, companies will be required to pay within nine months of the end of the accounting period. Previously, companies had sometimes been permitted to delay their payment of Corporation Tax for up to 21 months. By 1992 companies will be required to run a 'Pay and File' system of payment for Corporation Tax which will involve automatic and harsh penalties for any tax paid late.

Advance Corporation Tax

If a company pays a dividend to its shareholders it must pay tax at $^{27}/_{73}$ of the dividend payment. An amount equal to 27% of the Advance Corporation Tax (ACT) charge can be deducted from a company's liability to corporation tax and can, sometimes, eliminate the liability altogether. Few private incorporated companies award dividends, although it can sometimes pay the directors to take their remuneration in dividends rather than salary, so the effect of the ACT offset on Corporation Tax should not be overlooked. Recently, the restriction which meant ACT could not be offset against that part of Corporation Tax which comes from capital gains has been removed.

Capital Gains Tax

Capital Gains Tax (CGT) is charged whenever you dispose of an asset at a profit. The tax is charged only on the profit made – not on the total value of the asset when it is sold.

CGT is payable by individuals operating as sole traders or in partnerships just as much as it is by incorporated companies. At the time of writing, individuals are exempt from CGT up to an annual level of gains of £6,600.

In an incorporated business CGT is charged to Corporation Tax and today the distinction which used to exist between capital gains profits and profits from income has been dropped (see above). This means a company can be assessed for CGT at the small companies Corporation Tax rate of 27%, if its profits are below the required level of £100,000.

CGT is payable on a wide range of transactions. If a partner sells out his share of the partnership his gain can attract CGT. If you sell the freehold of your business premises, or even a leasehold before it expires, this will be liable for CGT. Gains on the sale of small items of plant with values of below £3,000 do not attract tax. It is possible to reduce the size of your taxable gain by charging certain costs. For example, if you have sold a property on which you had previously carried out extension work, this could be deductible against CGT. But this would not apply if you had previously charged that extension work as a capital allowance.

If you are self-employed or in a partnership and replacing business assets you can sometimes 'roll over' any CGT liability by deducting the gain on the old asset from the price of the new one. The same relief is available to incorporated businesses where a family has 50% of the votes or you personally control 25% of the votes.

If you sell your business upon retirement, CGT once again enters the picture, but you may be entitled to 'retirement relief' of up to £125,000 to reduce your liability. This would apply to a share of a partnership, shares in the family company or an asset which has been used rent-free by your own or your family's business.

If you decide to turn your sole-tradership or partnership into an incorporated business, CGT arises because in the eyes of the law the limited business is a separate legal entity to which you have sold an asset. This is not quite the burden it sounds because you can defer your CGT liability until you eventually dispose of your shares in the company. But you have to sell the whole company with all its assets as a going concern if this tactic is to work.

PAYE

Once you take on an employee (perhaps just your spouse), whose income exceeds certain limits and when the Tax Office tells you to use a certain code, you are obliged to make deductions through the Pay As You Earn system (see chapter 16). In the tax year 1987/88 the earnings thresholds above which PAYE apply are payments of £45 a week or £195 a month. If you are employing people being paid these amounts, you must obtain the Inland Revenue's *Employer's Guide to PAYE* which will guide you through the many complexities involved.

The PAYE deductions system works alongside the system for National Insurance contributions and the Inland Revenue's Deductions Working Sheets permit for the calculation of both.

Legal requirements say you must:
- Operate PAYE if you are in any doubt about the tax position of anyone you employ.
- Pay at the end of each month any tax and National Insurance contributions which you have collected to the Inland Revenue's Accounts Office.
- Permit Inland Revenue and DHSS officers to inspect your PAYE and National Insurance contribution records if they ask.

- Keep the following records for at least three years: Pay Records; Deductions Working Sheets; any P46 forms that you have not sent to the Tax Office.

Each time you pay an employee you must:
- Work out the employee's pay.
- Work out how much pay the employee must pay tax on using the employee's tax code and tax tables.
- Work out the tax the employee has to pay.
- Record any Statutory Sick Pay and Statutory Maternity Pay.
- Record all tax deducted or returned to the employee.
- Record National Insurance Contributions.

Within 14 days of the end of each tax month you must pay the Inland Revenue's Accounts Office all tax and National Insurance contributions, including those contributions made as an employer (see chapter 16 for details) having first:
- Deducted any gross Sick Pay.
- Deducted any gross Maternity Pay.
- Deducted an amount to compensate for the employer's National Insurance on any Statutory Sick Pay.
- Deducted an amount to compensate for the employer's National Insurance paid on Statutory Maternity Pay.

At the end of a tax year you must send the Inspector a return (P14) for each employee. This will include details of:
- The employee's total pay during that year.
- Total tax deducted during the year.
- The employee's National Insurance number and details of employee's and employer's contributions during the year.
- Total Statutory Sick Pay and Statutory Maternity Pay made during the year.

Remember that a wide range of income counts as pay for tax purposes, and can include all salaries, fees, bonuses, commissions, Christmas gifts, sick and maternity pay, vouchers, travel pay, lump sum payments and tips and service charges paid by the employer.

Even if you operate your PAYE system through a computer bureau you must pay heed to the various requirements set out under the Income Tax (Employments) Regulations. The Inland Revenue has stepped up the number of PAYE audits it carries out on companies. These can include searching reviews of many of the aspects of employing people. For example: the accuracy of PAYE deductions sheets, use of employee code numbers, cash payments where PAYE has not been operated and procedures dealing with employees' expenses.

Typical difficulties on PAYE audits arise in areas like:

- Gross payments to casual employees.
- Gross payments to people who profess to be self-employed.
- Private petrol.
- Employee expenses, such as entertaining.
- Travel for other than business purposes.
- Use of home telephones.
- Expenses for using home as an office.

The treatment of casual labour and people who claim to be self-employed are probably the two biggest problem areas encountered by many businesses during a PAYE audit. The basic rule is that if an employee is either going to earn pay above the PAYE threshold in a given week or above the National Insurance lower earnings limit (see chapter 16), you should prepare a deductions working sheet for him or her.

The IR also occasionally makes investigations into the business accounts of self-employed people and small companies. If you keep full and up-to-date records these investigations can be completed fairly quickly. Otherwise they may take months. The Inland Revenue says the sort of things which encourage it to make an investigation are:

- A level of profits lower than a similar business in the area.
- An amount taken out from the business which is clearly not enough for you to live on.
- Unusually high business expenses.
- New funds being put into the business when it is unclear where they came from.
- Savings which have grown faster than expected, given the profits of your business.
- Information from elsewhere (i.e. your bank account) which does not agree with your tax return.

Penalties for offences on tax matters can be adjusted according to your degree of co-operation and the seriousness of the offence. But the IR can seek penalties for:

- Failing to tell the IR when you start in business and become liable for tax (up to £100 for each tax year).
- Sending in a tax return late (up to £50, or if there is a very long delay, £50 plus the amount of tax involved).
- Understating profits or gains on your tax return or accounts, or making incorrect claims for tax relief (up to £50 plus the amount of tax in case of negligence, up to twice the amount of tax plus £50 in cases of fraud).

14. Insurance and pensions

Whatever your business is, it is essential that it is protected by insurance. Some types of insurance, such as that for vehicles and equipment and the covering of employee safety, is required by law while others, like those dealing with fire damage or personal cover for the entrepreneur and his or her family, are optional.

The degree of cover you obtain for your business will depend on the extent to which you are at risk from break-ins, damage, loss etc. Don't ignore the need for adequate insurance. All you may have built up could be lost in an instant unless you have had the foresight to protect your own interests.

It is impossible to generalise about a business's insurance requirements. The big insurance companies offer so many different types of insurance packages for businesses that it is usually possible to tailor arrangements to meet your own special needs. The important thing is to find a reputable insurance broker who specialises in business insurance. Your accountant can advise you on finding an insurance broker if you are unsure which one to select. Usually, dealing with an insurance broker is preferable to going direct to the insurance company. A broker will charge the insurance company, rather than you, so his services are normally free. The broker is also in close touch with the market and able to quote the best prices. He is also able to help with claims and generally save some of your own precious time.

Compulsory insurance

Employer's liability: In accordance with the Employer's Liability (Compulsory Insurance) Act 1969 any business which has employees must provide them with insurance cover for death or injury during work. The cover will be to protect you against any damages which may be brought against you. The legal requirement is for all firms to have a minimum of £2 million of protection although there is usually no upper limit involved. Premiums are set as a percentage of your business's sales.

Vehicle policy: Ordinary personal insurance cover on a vehicle will be inadequate when it is being used for business purposes. You will be required to obtain a commercial-use policy.

Inspections: Some items of equipment like boilers, lifts and hoists have, by law, to be regularly inspected. An insurance company is allowed to perform this inspection and appropriate cover can be obtained for this purpose. If you don't provide insurance for inspections, another 'competent person' will provide the inspection for a fee and issue the necessary certificate of worthiness.

General business insurance

The type of eventualities which a business must insure itself against will vary according to the type of business and its location. In the case of 'business assets' the type of risks will include:

- Explosions
- Fire
- Burst pipes
- Riot/civil disturbances
- Flood
- Vehicle impact
- Aircraft accidents

You can restrict the amount of cover to certain categories depending on the degree of exposure or remoteness to the risk. When fixing the amount of cover you can opt for either an 'indemnity' or 'reinstatement' basis.

Indemnity cover merely insures assets at their current market value. This is probably the type of insurance you would require if you knew that after loss or damage you would not be replacing those assets. Reinstatement allows you to recover the full replacement cost of buildings and equipment or the total cost of repair after damage.

Just insuring your business assets will provide insufficient recompense in the event of damage or loss. While your property is being replaced or repaired the effect on your profits could be disastrous. This is why businesses take out 'consequential loss' insurance. A business should try to insure itself against consequential loss for a period of at least one year. Your accountant will need to help the insurance company assess the future likely profitability of your business. Consequential loss insurance can be extended to cover things like goods-in-transit or damage at your customers' or suppliers' premises.

If you run a business handling large amounts of cash you may have to obtain separate 'fidelity' cover to guard against theft and fraud on the part of your employees. Exposure to danger from people outside your company can be covered by a normal 'theft' insurance policy.

Other relevant insurances include those which cover 'stock' (both raw materials and finished goods), 'public liability' (protects you against damages brought by a third party being injured or damaged on your property), 'credit insurance' (covers losses made through insolvency or payment default of customers), and 'legal expenses' insurance (can be essential to pay the fees for any litigation in which you may be involved).

Health insurance

The fortunes of most small companies are usually dependent on just one person or a small handful of people. The effect of one of these people becoming ill or dying can be catastrophic. There are many different health insurance packages which can defend your business against this eventuality.

Even if you just operate on your own as self-employed you should consider taking out life assurance cover for your family to provide for them if you were to die. A 'Permanent Health Insurance' (PHI) plan to replace lost income if you fall ill can be important. Sometimes this can be the difference between your business closing down or continuing.

Life assurance and PHI are relatively cheap for self-employed people, although it is surprising how few take advantage of the covers available. Life assurance, which can be linked to your pension arrangements (see below) can be obtained either as a lump sum payment to your family on your death or as a series of monthly payments. The self-employed can claim income tax relief against their life assurance contributions at their highest tax rate.

PHI schemes can be constructed to suit your own requirements but, along with National Insurance they normally permit replacement of around 75% of your income at a set time, say three months, after disablement. A PHI policy could contribute towards the cost of employing a replacement manager for your business, although this won't always be practicable. The terms of a PHI policy are such that if disablement was permanent you would have the comfort of receiving income right up to retirement age (when you start receiving pension payments).

Key man cover

In small companies where there might be just a few people who generate a large part of the business's income, special 'key man' life cover can be obtained against his or her death or illness. Key man policies set maximum benefits and restrict the period in which they can be paid after disability. If the key man dies, a lump sum is payable to the business. The cost of this type of cover is not expensive when you consider the damage which could be done to a business through the loss of a vital director or executive. A five-year policy providing £100,000 worth of cover can be obtained for premiums of below £300 a year.

In the case of partnerships special types of insurance are available which protect the business in the event of death or illness. Life assurance can be arranged on the partners' lives so that the shares of one partner who has died can be bought out by the other partners.

Sometimes it can pay the directors of a company to take out 'group life and health cover' for themselves and all, or most, of their employees. There are many such schemes on the market today and premiums are competitive. Group cover schemes ask fewer questions about personal health, and there may be no distinction between smokers and non-smokers. In small close knit companies where there is a need to keep morale high, there can be genuine benefits from offering the incentive of group life cover as a perk.

Pensions for the self-employed

As a self-employed person or partner in a business you are only entitled to the State Pension Benefit when you retire. But the State allows you to obtain tax relief on the premiums paid into any private pension scheme so, for higher rate taxpayers in particular, such schemes make sound economic sense. If you were a 60% rate taxpayer and paid premiums of £1,500 a year into your pension fund your tax relief would amount to £900 a year, so your net outlay would be only £600 a year. But because there is no tax payable on the investment income and gains on approved scheme pensions, the fund has your £1,500 which is earning you tax free income all the time.

It is also possible to 'bring forward' unused tax relief on pension contributions from the previous six years and then apply it to tax rates for the current year.

Indeed, pension schemes are one of the most tax-efficient investments for the individual so anyone who is self-employed should start making contributions to a private scheme as early as possible. The tax regime for all pension schemes is in the process of change and, despite delays, is moving towards a situation where private pension schemes will be fully 'portable'. This means you can maintain payments into your own scheme regardless of whether you later become an employee of a company with its own pension arrangements. This should encourage more self-employed people to take out private schemes early on, rather than delay because of the fear that they may have to suspend payments into their own scheme at a later stage. The amount you are allowed to invest in a pension scheme is defined as a percentage of your net 'relevant earnings'. If you had an income of £20,000 and £4,000 of expenses, then your net relevant income would be £16,000. After 4th January 1988 tax relief is available on contributions up to these maximum limits:

Age	% of earnings
50 or less	17.5
51–55	20.0
56–60	22.5
61–75	27.5

The variety and flexibility of private pension schemes is now very impressive. Most schemes now allow you to take your pension in a series of regular payments, or as a lump sum plus regular payments. The tax free lump sum must not exceed 25% of the value of the fund on retirement.

Unit-linked pension plans permit you to have a say in which markets your premiums will be invested. It is possible to switch your investment from one fund, or a combination of funds, to another. Additional flexibility is in the pipeline which will do away with the limits on benefits which can be taken by the age of 50, and those which must be taken by age 75.

In choosing a pension scheme you should pay attention to a fund's past performance. This is the only guide you have to what you can expect your final pension to be worth. Depending on how early you have started paying premiums, the total value of a personal pension fund can be staggeringly high when you retire.

Pension schemes can have the additional advantage of being used as the basis for a business loan. The loan would depend on the value of your fund and, although it would attract interest, this would be fully allowable against tax as a normal business loan.

Pensions for directors

Unless you are going to run a company-wide pension scheme for directors and staff there is no reason why, as a director, you can't take out a private pension in the same way as a self-employed person. But in the case of a small incorporated company, with just a handful of key directors and executives, there are a number of tailor-made 'executive' pension schemes on the market which are well worth considering because they offer tax advantages to both the company and the individual.

In funding an executive pension you have the choice of running either an 'insured' scheme or a 'self-administered' scheme. With an insured scheme the contributions are paid over to the insurance company responsible for investing your money. This keeps the fund separate from the company, but can mean less flexibility in taking full advantage of available tax savings.

In a self-administered scheme the directors can exercise considerable control over how the money is invested. The setting up costs can be high, but readily available funds mean that you might be able to invest the pension money in the company itself, perhaps by buying the company's offices or purchasing shares in the company.

Some insurance firms offer the opportunity to combine the advantages of both the insured and self-administered schemes by making your company's directors trustees of the fund, as long as an outside trustee with experience of pension matters is also appointed.

As a director you are an employee of your own company and to launch an approved pension scheme your company must make a contribution to the fund. Provided the benefits of the pension scheme do not exceed Inland Revenue limits, there is no ceiling on the company's funding of the scheme. As a pension fund member, however, your contributions cannot exceed 15% of your earnings. It will be apparent that this is a very flexible arrangement for a director and is, indeed, one of the main advantages of the incorporated company.

With an executive pension scheme you will be able to raise or reduce your contributions as it suits you. You could stop paying all contributions for a while if your business's fortunes demand it, or even top up the fund with lump sum payments. Because the employer's contributions can be offset against tax it also provides enormous scope for reducing, or even eliminating, your liability to Corporation Tax.

Pension schemes also usually have an extra facility which allows you to add life cover to protect your family if you die. Some schemes will allow you to vary what proportion of your contributions go to make up the life cover, and you can adjust this to suit your personal circumstances.

15. Business premises

Finding suitable premises has never been easy for the self-starter in business. Even today, when there is a great deal of government and local authority assistance, it can often seem that there is every type of property except the one you want.

People setting up business are often reluctant to move far in order to find premises. This means that there can be industrial and commercial space going begging in areas like Enterprise Zones, where there is special assistance (see chapter 17), but seemingly little in other places where demand for property is higher. Of course, many people starting up their own business elect to sell to their local community. So moving their base far away will rarely be an option. But there can often be considerable advantages to locating a start-up business where there are custom-made facilities for small firms, together with generous financial incentives.

Working from home

Many small businesses which have later grown into large and successful companies have started in the spare room, garage or garden shed of a private dwelling. This is the logical choice for many people whose business does not require much space, and who are unlikely to be taking on employees for a while. There are usually few problems involved in using your home as a base for business, but there can sometimes be difficulties with planning regulations, the payment of rates and your building society if you have a mortgage. Questions to ask are:

Do I need planning permission? Local authorities will usually have little objection if you are just using one room of a house for business purposes. As long as there is not a queue of cars outside, lorries continually pulling up or unusual noises disturbing the neighbourhood you should be in the clear. The planning controls incorporated in the various Town and Country Planning Acts start to take effect when there is a material 'change of use' in the property. Certainly any physical alteration to your property to accommodate the business must first be cleared with the local authority. Also, if the business starts to become the principal use of the property, planning permission should be obtained.

Is it best to ask about planning permission first? It is certainly worth finding out about the policy of your local authority. You can review planning policies at your local authority offices and these will probably give you a good guide as to whether your proposals are going to upset the planning strategy. You can also talk to the planning department if you need further clarification. It is possible to make an application for a determination of your position on planning regulations which could prevent the local authority taking tough action over your business at a later stage. If, for any reason, planning permission is refused you are free to appeal. This can be worth the effort because many planning appeals are successful and they are not expensive to pursue.

Should I tell my building society? Yes. In some house deeds there are restrictive covenants prohibiting use of the property for business purposes. In some circumstances using your home for business could affect your buildings and contents insurance.

What expenses will I be able to claim against tax? Most household bills like gas, electricity, rates and telephone can be deducted against tax if you are using your home for business. But the amount you can claim has to be in proportion to how much of the house you have used for business purposes. If you are using one-fifth of the property for business, you will usually be allowed to set one-fifth of your bills against tax. Because you are not using all your home for residential purposes, however, you can lose the freedom from Capital Gains Tax when you sell your house. Your CGT liability would be in proportion, again, to how much of the home was used for business. You should discuss this detail with your accountant to see if it could become a major problem later.

Looking for premises

Consider the following points if you are beginning a search for suitable office or factory accommodation.

Allow sufficient time. Finding business premises is just as time consuming as looking for residential property, possibly even more so. You should start the search process very early in your planning phase and certainly not expect to move in until at least six months after you have finally found somewhere to your liking. If possible, have your finance arranged early and get your solicitor working on the legal details straight away.

Where to look. High street estate agents handle commercial property and you should inform them of your requirements and ask them to post you details of potentially suitable premises, in the same way as looking for a new house. Local newspapers also regularly advertise business premises.

There is much government help for small firms seeking property, so it is a good idea to begin any search at your local authority. Ask the Estates Department about the availability of small workshop schemes, enterprise agency or business club property programmes, or of any converted buildings with 'nursery units'. If you live in or near an Enterprise Zone, make direct enquiries about space for small businesses.

You should be as entrepreneurial in looking for premises as you plan to be in your business. Just imagine how many factories and offices there are in your area which have a tiny corner, a desk, a room or small piece of factory floorspace which they might let you use for a modest rent? It's worth asking.

Other possible sources of help include: the government-sponsored English Estates, which builds premises up to 2,500 sq ft and offers special tenancy and rental agreements; the Council for Small Industries in Rural Areas (CoSIRA) which encourages enterprise in country areas; British Steel Corporation (Industry) which provides workshop space in areas hit by the closure of steel-making plants.

How much space do I require? This is never an easy question for a start-up business to answer because it has little notion of how fast it will expand. Many businesses which start out in special nursery units find they have to move out to larger premises within a year. Moving is costly, time consuming and should be done as little as possible. On the other hand, start-up businesses don't usually have the cash to acquire a large amount of space unless part of their premises can be sub-let to another business.

You should sketch out your office or factory layout and try to determine precisely where everything you need is going to fit. Don't forget storage space for stocks, finished items etc. This way you can calculate your floorspace needs and tell your estate agent exactly what you require. If you are setting up a small jobbing engineering business you may find that you need no more than 2,500 sq ft – little more than a typical lock-up garage. This can be the most difficult size of property to acquire, so you may want to anticipate expansion and go for something larger. Make sure that the space you are being sold is all useable, because the rent will usually relate to the total space even though some of it may be impossible to use for production purposes.

What type of property? You should make a list of what you need from a property before you buy or rent, rather than be dissatisfied later and find you have to pay for costly refurbishment and alterations or, even worse, a move. Things to avoid if possible are: restricted parking and vehicle access, buildings with partitions, lack of insulation, poor lighting, shared facilities (unless in special small firm workshop or nursery-unit developments), excess noise or disturbance from adjoining businesses and limited headroom or floor loading capacity. You should, in particular, check that the property meets the requirements of the Health and Safety at Work Act.

A modern factory or office is definitely preferable to an old one. They are invariably better designed, cheaper to run and won't need special refurbishment or renovation. Custom-made small business workshops are often the best option. Typically, there are shared facilities for things like the telephone switchboard, receptionist, mailing etc. To be close to other like-minded souls in new businesses is not bad for the morale either, and on some such developments the businesses even trade with each other. Very often there are arrangements for the acquisition of additional space as businesses expand, and sometimes business advisory services are on hand.

Freeholds, leases and rents

If at all possible, a business should usually buy the freehold of its property rather than take a lease and pay rent. A freehold can be a valuable and appreciating asset and is particularly attractive now that rent reviews tend to occur more frequently. But few start-up businesses have the capital to buy a property and a business would need a few years trading before it could obtain a mortgage.

Never take on a lease without advice from your solicitor and surveyor. Certainly, there will be fewer problems if you are taking a leasehold on a new property. On old properties you may find yourself taking on all sorts of liabilities which you didn't expect.

For example, you will probably have to pay the landlord's property insurance and take responsibility for all repairs and maintenance of the property. Most landlords will try to enforce what is called a 'full repairing and insurance liability' on you. Resist this, but if you can't avoid it make sure that there is nothing wrong with the building when you take on the lease. It is important to have a surveyor check the building before you sign the agreement.

Also check that there are no restrictions on the use of the property. Sometimes you might find that planning permission for the building has only been granted for a certain type of business use. Ask whether you are allowed to sub-let, what the service charges are and when the rent reviews are due.

Rent reviews can come as frequently as the landlord likes and he can charge what he pleases. It is up to you to determine whether he is asking a competitive rent for this type of property and area. As you would expect, rent levels are lower in the north, but there is rarely a 'cheap' rent these days. Even in assisted areas, like Enterprise Zones, rent levels can seem little cheaper than elsewhere. The advantage of some Enterprise Zones is that they can sometimes offer rent and rate-free periods which assist a business's cash-flow in the early stages.

Leasehold agreements can vary a lot in what they say about rent reviews. Sometimes they can link rent increases to the inflation rate – tough in times of high inflation. If you can, seek a rent review clause which puts a ceiling or percentage limit on the increase. Ask your surveyor for guidance on likely rent levels in the next few years when you take on the lease.

When a lease ends, the conditions of the Landlord and Tenants Act 1954 allow you to stay in the premises until you have been offered a new lease. The landlord will have to give you six months' notice of termination and you would have to respond within two months whether you wanted to go or accept the new terms.

Rates

If VAT is a small business's biggest hate, the rates don't come far behind. Rates can be a very major item in a small company's overheads and this makes it important to establish likely rate changes early on in your business planning (see chapter 4). You are only going to be free of rates in Enterprise Zones, so don't underestimate their impact on your business costs. Rates are something of a political football, and their impact on business is even more contentious since the proposed introduction of a poll tax.

When you draw up your business plan the chances are that you have not yet moved into premises and are unaware of ratable values. But do some research beforehand and ask the local authority what rates are being paid by businesses with floor space comparable to that in your own plans. Remember that rates are one of your most variable costs. Almost anything can happen to rates, depending on the political complexion of your local authority. Up until about 1984 rates were rising twice as fast as inflation. And there are enormous geographical variations which make a nonsense of fair competition between businesses. A business in the south of England could be paying rates 30 times higher than a comparable business in the north.

Rate appeals are certainly worth considering by small business people aggrieved by what they see as unreasonable demands. The rates you pay are made up of two parts: a rating assessment determined by the Inland Revenue and a rate-in-the-pound determined by the local authority to cover its anticipated expenditure. It is far easier to appeal against the rating assessment than the rate-in-the-pound. Put simply, you have to put a case to your local Valuation Officer (you can do this yourself or use a rating surveyor who will charge a fee) which proves that you are paying too much relative to similar commercial properties, or that since the last valuation something has happened to the property which means it should have a lower ratable value. For example, if a motorway has been built which seriously detracts from the customer-access to your business, you probably have good cause for an appeal. In the most recent rate revaluations some rating surveyors achieved reductions in 75% of the cases they handled.

Moving in

The first item that may need attention once you have finally signed your lease is some kind of conversion work to adapt the premises to your needs. Planning permission will be required for practically any change. Even a new shop front requires planning permission. You may need to get a 'change of use certificate' if you are, say, converting premises from light industrial use to retail use. All this takes time, so apply early. And don't forget, many businesses underestimate the amount of time involved in setting up and consequently underestimate their financial requirements.

If you are contemplating conversion work, consider the cost involved compared with what you are going to get back in return. If you are planning to move out of the premises in a few years it hardly pays to spend thousands making a specialist conversion. You will need an architect as well as a builder and surveyor for most conversions. Watch out for legal requirements too – there are laws stating how much space should be allowed per worker. This applies to shops as well as factories.

Furnishing and equipping may sound like the easiest part of setting up a business. After all, all you must do, surely, is buy some secondhand desks and chairs etc. But equipping a business needs planning. Computers, word processors and telexes can be just as relevant to a small business as to a large one and you should try to anticipate your needs in a few years' time, rather than think just in terms of what you need on day one. Flexibility is vital.

Buying, leasing and hire purchase

Outright purchase of plant and equipment is not necessarily the best idea from a financial point of view. Tax relief on capital expenditure is no longer so extensive and interest on bank loans is variable and difficult to plan for. You will also be using up some of your available borrowing facilities and getting deeper into the mire of personal bank guarantees.

The alternative is leasing or hire purchase. In a lease, the lessee (you) takes possession of the item in return for a set rental over a defined period. Unlike a bank loan, the repayments do not vary and there is no repayment of capital. When the lease expires it is often the case that the lessor will permit you to resume the lease at a cheaper rental. Leasing is extremely flexible and agreements can be tailored to meet your needs. On the other hand, if you lease equipment which becomes out-of-date or obsolete you are stuck with the item, or the payments, until the lease expires. You can, however, sell the item on to a third party at the end of a lease, sharing the larger part of the secondhand price with the leasing company.

With hire purchase agreements you pay through instalment credit and take ownership of the item at the end of the period in return for a small sum. Hire purchase agreements are probably more easily obtained than leasing arrangements, but interest rates are generally more expensive than on bank loans.

Whether you buy, lease or opt for hire purchase depends on the individual circumstances of your business. Leasing has grown in popularity with businesses over the years, but there is pressure on leasing rates and you should make a thorough assessment of the competition before signing an agreement.

Energy management

The last thing you may think of when you move into business premises is how long the lights are switched on for, or whether the heating thermostat is set too high. Energy is a fixed cost which can be substantially reduced – by as much as a third – simply by devoting some thought to the matter.

Give the same attention to insulation, draughts and floor coverings as you would in a residential property. Also, check with the electricity and gas boards that you are paying the business rate. The Department of Energy will be happy to advise you on ways to save on heating and lighting bills. Savings made here can be crucial in the vital trimming of costs needed to achieve a more competitive price for your product or service (see chapter 6).

16. Employing staff

Most people who start out in business on their own are filled with dread at the thought of taking on their first employee. The tax, National Insurance and a tangle of employment law all add up to a big headache which, regrettably, prevents some small businesses expanding as they should. Belatedly, the Government has woken up to the fact that small businesses are a major force in job creation, and that by simplifying the bureaucratic detail, they may encourage firms to take on more staff.

The Department of Employment has been trying to de-regulate some of the complexities involved in taking on employees and you should contact your local Small Firms Centre (Tel: 100 ask for *Freefone Enterprise*), Jobcentre or Unemployment Benefit Office to keep pace with developments in this area. Broadly, firms now employing less than 20 people will find that in certain matters the laws have been relaxed. To start with you should obtain the leaflet entitled *Taking Someone On* which sets out the essentials in 10 areas of the law, including trade union membership, maternity rights, contracts of employment and unfair dismissal. The Department of Employment has also produced a set of fact sheets on Employment Law.

Taking on your wife or husband

If you are self-employed your spouse will very often be your first employee. Sometimes this will be in an unpaid capacity but it is worth bearing in mind that any salary you pay to your spouse will be tax deductible as a genuine trading cost. You should pay the salary, drawn by cheque from the business account.

How much you pay your spouse will depend to some extent on your joint position for income tax. A wife's earned income allowance is currently £2,425 (1987/88) so anything she earns up to that level will be free of tax. If the two of you earn over £26,870 and your wife's earnings are in excess of £6,545, you will usually save tax by making a wife's 'earnings election' and taxing her separately.

Paying a salary of £39 per week (or £169 per month) and above, means you have to pay National Insurance contributions. As soon as income tax and National Insurance are being paid you enter the world of PAYE. This is the big change for anyone who has been operating as a one-person sole trader. Up to this point you will have probably been assessed at six-monthly intervals and paid tax in arrears on the entire profit of your business. You will continue to pay tax in this way for as long as you remain an unincorporated business, but you now have the additional paperwork and cost of a true employer.

Booklet IR53 *How to operate PAYE* is available from the Inland Revenue, and sets out the basic procedures involved in paying income tax in this way. The Revenue will also supply you with a PAYE number, a tax coding for your spouse and instruct you about making National Insurance payments. (See chapter 13 for more details on PAYE etc.)

Forming a partnership with your spouse

You may want to consider going into a proper business partnership with your spouse. This would meant that you both become jointly liable to the taxation of the partnership's profits (see chapter 2). You can, through the partnership agreement, decide to share the profits and losses of the partnership in a certain proportion between you. Income tax relief is now available on personal borrowings raised to make investments in partnerships, and relief is available on loans for partners buying plant and machinery. You will also pay less National Insurance because you will both be regarded as self-employed.

National Insurance

If you have been operating as a sole trader you will have been paying your Class 2 (fixed) and Class 4 (based on annual profits) National Insurance contributions in the same way as any self-employed person (see page 11). Both of these can be paid once a year, but when you take on an employee paying PAYE, National Insurance becomes at least a once-a-month detail requiring your attention.

Leaflet NP 15 *Employers' Guide to National Insurance Contributions*, obtainable free from any Social Security office, is essential reading.

The Department of Health and Social Security has endeavoured to make the calculation of National Insurance contributions as simple as possible. There are special tables and an official Deductions Working Sheet – P11 (87) – which you can use along with your PAYE calculations. If you are not automatically issued with a set of contributions tables, you can obtain them from your local Social Security office.

Employers pay National Insurance contributions for each member of staff. These start at 5% of salary on salaries between £169–281.99 per month and go up to 10.45% when the employee's salary exceeds £650 per month. Employees also start paying their contributions at a rate of 5%, but this goes up to 9% on salaries over £434 per month. Income of over £1,279 per month does not attract additional National Insurance from the employee, although there is no ceiling on employers' contributions.

As you can see, there are considerable savings to be made if you get the balance between salaries and National Insurance contributions right. Broadly speaking, it is better for National Insurance purposes to remain self-employed rather than form a limited company. In an incorporated business the company has to make a contribution as an employer and, as an employee drawing a salary from that company, you will have to make a further contribution.

However, as a self-employed person, if your business fails you will not be entitled to immediate unemployment benefits, or additional earnings-related pensions and widow's benefits.

If you form a limited company ask your accountant if you will be better off paying at least some of your own earnings in the form of dividends and thus avoiding any possible National Insurance charges.

Defining the job and training

What particular duties do you require your employee to perform? How much experience will he or she need? Do you require certain targets to be met – i.e. sales targets? Will there be a requirement for special skills such as book-keeping, driving, or the ability to use a small computer? It's surprising how few employers ever bother to define exactly what they require from an employee. This in turn is why so many employees have never really understood what is expected of them.

In a small firm the happiness of your employees is essential if your own drive and enthusiasm is to be successfully communicated. Write down your requirements, make sure these are stated in the job description at the time you advertise for an employee, and discuss them fully at the interview. You should also consider how much training you are going to provide for the employee. Many employees now expect a certain degree of formal training from employers. You may have to investigate what local authority or government schemes are available and whether any financial assistance is available. You may want to consider offering a place to someone on the Youth Training Scheme, sending someone on a government information technology course, or getting a grant towards the cost of retraining someone. Contact your local Jobcentre or the Manpower Services Commission Office for details of training opportunities.

Finding employees

Despite high unemployment levels, finding the right staff is never easy. Skill shortages abound in many areas and other types of jobs may simply be unpopular. Before you advertise or start searching for the right employee, consider the different recruiting sources.

Jobcentres: Very good for a wide range of occupations; offers ease and cheapness in finding suitable job candidates.

Employment agencies: Costly, but takes away some of the burden of finding employees.

Press advertising: Classified advertising of job vacancies is a quick and cheap way of reaching a mass audience. The newspaper can usually help you to find a suitable form of wording.

Educational establishments: If you are going to take on a regular number of new recruits every year it may pay to develop a relationship with local schools and colleges. This is time consuming, but probably worth it in terms of the quality of recruit.

Consultants: If you're looking for top executives, or even new partners, employment consultants are possibly the best source. Interviewing is done for you, but the fees are usually a percentage of first-year salary and can be expensive.

New Workers Scheme

Small businesses about to employ staff should consider taking advantage of the Government's New Workers Scheme (NWS) which is designed to help young people find jobs and make it easier for employers to create job openings. Employers can claim £15 per week if they provide a job for an under 21-year-old at a reasonable rate of pay. The NWS is basically designed to help people coming out of the Youth Training Scheme find their first job. The payment to employers lasts just one year. Minimum wages are laid down and you should check at a Careers Office or Jobcentre about the latest levels, as they are always under review.

Jobshare

Employers will sometimes find the government's Jobshare scheme very attractive. If you split an existing job, or even a new one, into two part-time jobs for unemployed people, you are entitled to receive £1,000 towards administration and training.

Employment contracts

A contract you make with an employee need not be in writing to be legally binding, but most employees are entitled to receive a written statement of the terms of the contract, within 13 weeks of their employment starting. The Department of Employment recommends that a written contract should include the following details:
- Names of the employer and employee.
- Job title.
- Date the employment began.
- Scale or rate of pay, or how pay is calculated.
- Intervals at which it is paid.
- Hours of work.
- Amount of holiday, including public holidays, and how holiday pay is calculated.
- Rules about absence due to sickness or injury including details of sick pay.
- Pension arrangements.
- Notice periods on both sides.
- Additional note setting out disciplinary rules and grievance procedures (except about health and safety at work) and saying who to contact if dissatisfied.

Some of the details above may not be relevant in all cases. Sometimes it would be sufficient to refer the employee to your company's rules or handbook. But some written statement should be given to the employee within 13 weeks of starting work. Any changes to the terms of employment should be notified to the employee within one month. The above will not be necessary for anyone working less than eight hours a week or those working between 8–16 hours a week who have not completed five years' continuous service. Useful booklets include:

- *Written Statement of Main Terms and Conditions of Employment* (DE1), from the Department of Employment.
- *Rules Governing Continuous Employment and a Week's Pay* (DE11), from the Department of Employment.
- *Industrial Tribunals Procedure* (DE ITL 1).
- *Employing People – The ACAS handbook for small firms*, available from ACAS regional offices.
- *Employers' Guide to Statutory Sick Pay* (N1227), from any Social Security office.

Pay statements and payroll procedures

If you anticipate expanding your staff numbers quite rapidly, talk to your bank manager about setting up an automated payroll procedure. These are quite sophisticated and take some of the administrative burden out of calculating PAYE deductions and National Insurance contributions (see pages 90 and 110).

Even if you employ just one person you are obliged to prepare itemised pay statements and a 'Standing Statement' every 12 months. The Department of Employment asks for itemised pay statements to state:

- The gross wage or salary.
- Details of fixed deductions.
- Amounts of, and reasons for, variable deductions.
- The net wage or salary (take-home pay).
- If an employee's net wage or salary is paid in more than one way (for example, part in cash and the rest by cheque) the pay statement must say how much is being paid by each method.

The annual Standing Statement must show:

- The amounts of, and reasons for, each fixed deduction and the total for fixed deductions.
- The intervals at which each fixed deduction is made.

Again, the above will not apply to staff working less than eight hours a week or those working between 8–16 hours a week who have not completed five years' continuous service.

114

Useful booklets include:
- *Itemised Pay Statements* (DE 8), from the Department of Employment.
- *The Law on the Payment of Wages and Deductions – a Guide to Part 1 of the Wages Act 1986*, from the Department of Employment.

Employees and the law

The Health and Safety at Work Act 1974 lays down the guidelines for looking after your employees' physical wellbeing at the workplace. It is worth becoming familiar with the requirements placed upon you as an employer by this Act and you can obtain advice from your local office of the Health and Safety Executive.

Today, firms employing less than 20 employees are given a little more room when it comes to implementing everything in this Act. Such firms, for example, will not have to comply with the requirement to prepare a written safety policy.

Manufacturing businesses have to be the most watchful in areas of health and safety. The need to ensure that plant and machinery are safe and regularly maintained is an obvious concern, but adequate lighting and ventilation, proper access and fire escape facilities and protection against dangerous fumes, must all be given attention.

Any accidents which occur on your premises must be notified to the relevant authority as soon as possible. This is often your local authority but varies depending upon the type of business.

Other areas of legal concern to any business will include:
Unfair dismissal: The government is attempting to ease the legislative burden on small firms in this area. Employees who believe they have been unfairly dismissed can complain to an industrial tribunal within three months of their dismissal, provided they have worked for their ex-employer for at least two years.
Redundancy: Employees have the right to redundancy payments after two years' service when they have been working for 16 hours a week or more. The payment is statutarily based on age, length of service and weekly pay. On occasions the Department of Employment will make the redundancy payment if the firm concerned cannot pay. The firm, in this case, would then be required to pay the money back at a later stage, probably in

instalments. Firms employing fewer than 10 employees can obtain a redundancy rebate of 35% of the statutory payment.

Maternity: Employed women who become pregnant have the right to paid time off for ante-natal care, to receive maternity pay and to return to work after maternity absence. The calculation of maternity pay is now dealt with under the Statutory Maternity Pay scheme. An employee has the right to return to her old job at any time up to 29 weeks beginning the week in which the baby is born. Firms with five or less employees may waive a woman's right to return to work if it is not reasonably practical for the company.

Paternity: Paternity leave is at the discretion of the employer.

Dismissal: Employees are normally entitled to a notice period if they are dismissed and they can ask for written reasons for their dismissal. Notice periods must be:

- One week when employment has been between one month and two years.
- One week for each completed year when employment has been between 2 to 12 years. 12 weeks when employment has been for more than 12 years.

Union membership: Employees have the right to join or not to join a trade union. A closed shop does not alter the right of a person not to join the union unless this has been supported in a secret ballot and received 80% support of those affected.

Secret ballots: Unions must hold secret ballots to elect their executives. If they do not hold secret ballots on the issue of strike action they may lose their immunity under the law. If a secret ballot has not been held, employers may apply for an injunction to call off the strike and claim damages up to £250,000.

Time off work: An employer must give time off work for various public positions and duties including trade union duties and legal and local authority duties.

Sick pay

Since 1983 every employer is responsible for paying Statutory Sick Pay (SSP), except in certain circumstances, for up to eight weeks of sickness absence in each tax year. SSP is taxable and it also attracts National Insurance contributions. Businesses can, however, run their own sick pay schemes and thus meet their liability to SSP, either partially or wholly themselves. An employee receiving SSP would be able to reduce his or her income tax and National Insurance during the period of the benefit.

Holidays

There are no laws about how much holiday anyone can receive, but holiday periods for most full time employees are usually between two and six weeks.

The amount of holiday should be stated in the contract of employment and you should make sure the employee is aware of whether holiday can be carried forward into the next year or whether he or she is obliged to take the total entitlement in the same year.

17. Help and information

Willingness to seek information and help is one of the things which separates the successful entrepreneur from the unsuccessful. Amazingly, very few people going into self-employment bother to obtain any particular guidance whatsoever. This is a pity and, undoubtedly, one of the reasons why the small business failure rate is so high. Today there are so many different bodies offering help to the self-employed and small businesses that there should be no excuse for the entrepreneur being unable to obtain the assistance he or she needs. The following is a selection of key advisers to the self-employed and small businesses.

The government provides general advice and counselling services to both start-up and existing businesses through its Small Firms Service. Telephone *Freefone Enterprise* (dial 100) for details of your local Small Firms Centre. Other government help for businesses is also available through the:

Department of Trade and Industry,
1 Victoria Street,
London SW1H 0ET.
Tel: 01-215 5544

Industry Department for Scotland,
Alhambra House,
45 Waterloo Street,
Glasgow G2 6AT.
Tel: 041-248 2855

Welsh Office Industry Department,
Cathays Park,
Cardiff CF1 3NQ.
Tel: 0222 825111

Additional help for businesses in Scotland can be obtained through:

The Scottish Development Agency,
120 Bothwell Street,
Glasgow G2 7JP.
Tel: 041-248 2700

The Highlands and Islands Development Board,
Bridge House,
27 Bank Street,
Inverness IV1 1QR.
Tel: 0463 234171

Additional help for businesses in Wales can be obtained through:

The Welsh Development Agency,
Pearl House,
Greyfriars Road,
Cardiff CF1 3XX.
Tel: 0222 222666

Small businesses in Northern Ireland seeking help should contact:

The Local Enterprise Development Unit,
LEDU House,
Upper Galwally,
Belfast BT8 4TB.
Tel: 0232 491031

Additional help for small firms in rural areas can be obtained through:

Council for Small Industries in Rural Areas (CoSIRA),
141 Castle Street,
Salisbury,
Wiltshire SP1 3TP.
Tel: 0722 336255

Advice and support can be obtained from the many local
Enterprise Agencies. To discover your nearest agency contact
Business in the Community, telephone 01-253 3716, or in Scotland,
Scottish Business in the Community, telephone 031-334 9876.

If you are setting up a co-operative you should discover your
nearest agency by first contacting Co-operative Development
Agency, telephone 01-839 2988.

The government has created a number of Enterprise Zones in
many areas of England, Scotland, Wales and Northern
Ireland, where special incentives are available for small business
self-starters.

Further information on Enterprise Zones can be obtained from:

The Department of the Environment,
2 Marsham Street,
London SW1P 3EB.
Tel: 01-212 7158

In the designated 'New Towns' areas, assistance and incentives are available to all types of business. Further information is available from:

Commission for the New Towns,
Glen House,
Stag Place,
London SW1E 5AJ.
Tel: 01-828 7722

In areas where employment has been adversely affected by the closure of steel making operations BSC (Industry) provides extensive assistance to people wishing to start small firms. Contact:

BSC (Industry),
Ground Floor,
Canterbury House,
2-6 Sydenham Road,
Croydon CR9 2LJ.
Tel: 01-686 2311

Even if you are only just starting out in business it can be a good idea to join one of the small firm associations which offer a wide range of advice and counselling and, sometimes, special schemes to assist with legal expenses.

Three bodies which are as useful to the self-employed as to small companies are:

The Forum of Private Business,
Ruskin Chambers,
Drury Lane,
Knutsford,
Cheshire WA16 6HA.
Tel: 0565 4467

Alliance of Small Firms & Self-Employed People,
33 The Green,
Calne,
Wiltshire SN11 8DJ.
Tel: 0249 817003

The National Federation of Self-Employed and
Small Businesses,
32 St. Anne's Road,
West Lytham St. Anne's,
Lancashire FY8 1NY.
Tel: 0253 720911

Practically any type of business you set up will fall into a category
covered by a Trade Association. It is well worth considering joining
your relevant association. Their advice and literature could save
you much time in finding out information that is already easily
available. Trade associations are listed in The Directory of British
Associations, published by CBD Research, Beckenham, Kent.
Ask your local library.

Look in your telephone directory for your local Chamber of
Commerce or, if you are a retailer, Chamber of Trade. Both of
these bodies provide an invaluable source of advice on the local
business scene.

If you are interested in taking out a *franchise* business you can
check the worthiness of the particular franchise and obtain further
helpful advice and information by contacting the:

British Franchise Association,
Franchise Chambers,
75a Bell Street,
Henley-on-Thames,
Oxfordshire RG9 2BD.
Tel: 0491 578049

Businesses seeking agents should consult:

The British Agents Register,
24 Mount Parade,
Harrogate HG1 1BP.
Tel: 0423 60608

Manufacturers' Agents Association,
Lonsdale House,
7-11 High Street,
Reigate,
Surrey RH2 9AA.
Tel: 0737 240141

For advice on the raising of venture capital contact:

British Venture Capital Association,
1 Surrey Street,
London WC2R 2PS.
Tel: 01-836 5702

Investors in Industry,
91 Waterloo Road,
London SE1 8XP.
Tel: 01-928 7822

For any guidance you may need about the accountancy profession contact either of the following:

Institute of Chartered Accountants in England and Wales,
PO Box 433,
Chartered Accountants Hall,
Moorgate Place,
London EC2P 2BJ.
Tel: 01-628 7060

Institute of Chartered Accountants of Scotland,
27 Queen Street,
Edinburgh EH2 1LA.
Tel: 031-225 5673

Advice and information on all aspects of trade marks and patents is available from:

Institute of Trade Mark Agents,
Fourth Floor,
Canterbury House,
2-6 Sydenham Road,
Croydon CR0 9XE.
Tel: 01-686 2052

Institute of Patent Agents,
Staple Inn Buildings,
London WC1V 7PZ.
Tel: 01-405 9450

The Patent Office and Trade Marks Registry,
Patent Office,
State House,
66-71 High Holborn,
London WC1R 4TP.
Tel: 01-831 2525

For information about exporting:

British Overseas Trade Board,
1 Victoria Street,
London SW1H 0ET.
Tel: 01-215 7877

Information and advice on marketing and market research:

Institute of Marketing,
Moor Hall,
Cookham,
Maidenhead, Berkshire SL6 9QH.
Tel: 06285 24922

Market Research Society,
175 Oxford Street,
London W1R 1TA.

Industrial Market Research Association,
11 Bird Street,
Lichfield,
Staffordshire WS13 6PW.
Tel: 05432 263448

To register a company, contact:

Companies Registration Office,
Companies House,
55 City Road,
London EC1Y 1BB.
Tel: 01-253 9393

Companies Registration Office,
Companies House,
Crown Way,
Maindy,
Cardiff CF4 3UZ.
Tel: 0222 388588

Companies Registration Office,
102 George Street,
Edinburgh EH2 3DJ.
Tel: 031-225 5774

For advice on choosing and appointing an insurance broker:

British Insurance Brokers' Association,
BIBA House,
14 Bevis Marks,
London EC3A 7NT.
Tel: 01-623 9043

For information about factoring contact:

Association of British Factors,
147 Fleet Street,
London EC4A 2BU.
Tel: 01-583 0265

Guidance about design matters is available from:

The Design Council,
28 Haymarket,
London SW1Y 4SU.
Tel: 01-839 8000

Details of premises for small firms are available from:

English Estates North,
Methven House,
Kingsway,
Team Valley,
Gateshead,
Tyne and Wear NE11 0LN.
Tel: 091 4874711

For advice on choosing and appointing a solicitor to deal with your business affairs, contact:

The Law Society,
113 Chancery Lane,
London WC2A 1PL.
Tel: 01-242 1222

For advice on leasing contact:

Equipment Leasing Association,
18 Upper Grosvenor Street,
London W1X 9PB.
Tel: 01-491 2783

Information on training, and any available financial assistance can be obtained from:

Manpower Services Commission,
Moorfoot,
Sheffield S1 4PQ.
Tel: 0742 753275

Jobcentres:

See your local telephone directory.

For industrial relations details and advice contact:

ACAS,
11-12 St. James' Square,
London SW1Y 4LA.
Tel: 01-210 3600

Health and safety at work:

Health and Safety Executive,
Baynards House,
1 Chepstow Place,
Westbourne Grove,
London W2 4TF.
Tel: 01-221 0870

Taxation:

Inland Revenue – see your local telephone directory.

VAT:

Customs & Excise – see your local telephone directory for the nearest office.

Planning permissions, local premises and finance:

Local Authority – contact your local corporation or council.